BRIGHTON

...MORE THAN A GUIDE

JARROLD
Publishing

BRIGHTON

... MORE THAN A GUIDE

Acknowledgements
Photography © Jarrold Publishing by Neil Jinkerson.
Additional photography by kind permission of: Borde Hill Garden; British Engineerium Museum; Geraint Tellem; Glenda Clarke; Komedia; Regency Town House; The Royal Pavilion, Libraries & Museums, Brighton; Sea Life Centre; Walk of Fame, Weald and Downland Museum.

The quotes on pages 5 and 16 from *Brighton Rock* by Graham Greene are used by permission of Random House and David Higham Associates.

The publishers wish to thank Camay Chapman-Cameron for her invaluable assistance; also the many owners of Brighton businesses for their kindness in allowing us to photograph their premises.

All information correct at time of going to press but may be subject to change.

Printed in Singapore.
ISBN 0 7117 3592 1 1/05

Designer:
Simon Borrough
Editor:
Angela Royston
Artwork and walk maps:
Clive Goodyer
City maps:
© Brighton & Hove Visitor and Convention Bureau; mapping provided by Oxford Cartographers. The 'main routes' map on page 100 by The Map Studio Ltd, Romsey, Hants

Front cover:
Deckchairs on the beach

Title page:
Railings on Brighton Pier

CONTENTS

WELCOME TO BRIGHTON

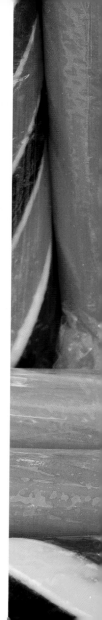

Ever since the enlightened Dr Richard Russell declared that sea water was good for your health, people have been flocking to Brighton to put the sparkle back into their lives. Back in 1750 the rich and fashionable came to its sunny shores to be 'dipped' in the restoring briny. Then the heir to the throne bought a simple farmhouse in this sunny Sussex town and Brighton hasn't looked back since.

Brighton Pier

The arrival of the Prince Regent with his fun-seeking entourage and his secret wife, Maria Fitzherbert, made Brighton the most desirable town in the whole of England. His farmhouse became an astonishing, many domed oriental palace and is still the city's best-known landmark.

BRIGHTON ROCK

'Brighton Rock is a form of sticky candy as characteristic of English seaside resorts as salt-water taffy is of the American. The word "Brighton" appears on the end of the stick at no matter what point it is broken off.' This explanation of our favourite seaside confectionery is given by the editor at the end of Graham Greene's book *Brighton Rock* – for the benefit of American readers.

BRIGHTON ROCK

BRIGHTON ROCK

Now Brighton, with its renowned shops and restaurants, entertainment and sheer seaside gaiety, is as fashionable and fun as ever. Dedicated shoppers say there's nowhere in the country to match it for sheer variety, while night owls can dance to a different tune every evening in the city's famous clubs. You may eat your way around the world in the hundreds of restaurants, or simply sit on the beach and watch the sunlight sparkling on the water.

Come for a day, a weekend or for a longer holiday. Wander in the ancient Lanes, marvel at the Royal Pavilion, stroll along the seafront, or take a turn on the pier. You'll find it's just what the doctor ordered.

Street musicians

Brighton Rocks (page 75)

Seagull on Brighton Pier

HIGHLIGHTS

As you step into the streets of Brighton for the first time, it's natural to feel like a child in a sweetshop. There are so many tempting things to do it's hard to know where to start. The shops or the beach? The Pavilion or the pier? Here are some of Brighton's top spots to get you started on this most invigorating of seaside cities.

The centre of Brighton itself is compact and easy to navigate on foot. Hove is a pleasant stroll along the seafront, while the Marina, to the east, is easily reached by bus, the little seafront electric railway, or on foot if you don't mind the 2-kilometre (1.25-mile) walk.

PAVILIONED IN SPLENDOUR

The Royal Pavilion (map E4) is a must-see, a one-off – Prinny's Palace by the sea. 'Prinny' was George, Prince of Wales, later the Prince Regent and, later still, King George IV. He turned a perfectly respectable farmhouse first into a neoclassical 'marine pavilion' and then, seized by desire for all things oriental, into a unique fantasy, all domes and turrets, dragons and lotus blossom.

TREAT YOURSELF

Visit the Royal Pavilion, which is jaw-droppingly gorgeous, and then treat yourself to a browse through their excellent shop, where you can buy the most lovely china and a wonderful selection of books about history, design, costume and Brighton itself.

The Royal Pavilion

The prince worked with architect John Nash and interior designers Frederick Crace and Robert Jones to produce the most extraordinary, most extravagantly sumptuous palace where he could have fun and entertain. It was completed in 1823, by which time George had been crowned king and had to take life more seriously. But music and dancing and entertaining and huge banquets were all the order of the day, until the glorious Pavilion was rejected by Queen Victoria, who much preferred solid Osborne House on the Isle of Wight and sold it to the town of Brighton in 1850.

Now the City of Brighton and Hove has done the Pavilion proud, recognizing it as one of its main assets. It's been superbly restored and you cannot help but gasp at the outrageous beauty of it all and marvel at the imagination that turned oriental fantasy into over-the-top reality.
Open: daily; Apr–Sep: 9.30–17.45 (last admission 17.00); Oct–Mar: 10.00–17.15 (last admission 16.30). Closed 25 and 26 Dec
Entry: under £10
Further information: pages 44–45

SEASIDE SPECIAL

Not one but two piers jut out into the Brighton waters. One is in-your-face, brash, chock-full of the latest amusement machines, the Dolphin Derby and funfair rides while still managing, underneath the flashing lights and thumping music, to retain its Victorian splendour.

The other, slowly sliding into the sea, has the dignity of an aristocratic old pile, sadly prey to the ravages of time and tide. It is a sorry sight, but somehow splendid in its decay. Visit Brighton Pier (map E6), eat candyfloss and cockles, stroll along the boardwalk and flop into a (free) deckchair to watch the waves and the sun slowly sinking over the broken West Pier (map A6) where nightly a huge flock of starlings comes home to roost.
Open: Brighton Pier: daily (weather permitting); summer: 9.00–2.00; winter: 10.00–21.30
Entry: free (there is a charge for amusements and rides)
Further information: page 39

Then there's the famous beach itself. Shingle piled high, shelving steeply towards the waves that suck and wash the stones back and forth. The area between the piers has a boardwalk to make progress across the shingle easy, cafés, restaurants, rides and plenty of entertainment for children. As night falls, the clubs along this stretch begin to throb with evening excitement. If all this is not too much for one visit, you can do the obvious thing and test the temperature of the bracing waves. If you like to bare all, the nudist beach by The Marina is clearly marked – a neat shingle wall hides all-over sunbathers from curious public view.

Brighton Pier

SPECIALLY FOR SHOPPERS

Even the most hardened shopaholics will find a new spring in their step and a gleam in their eye at the contemplation of the extraordinary mix of retail outlets in Brighton's main shopping areas. For years The Lanes had it – no contest. The Lanes (map D5) are still wonderful – twisty turning passageways, enhanced by picturesque twittens and catcreeps (connecting alleyways) and made beautiful by the sheer number and variety of shops. Jewellery of all types dominates here and, if you have something specific in mind, you'll find it. Now, after a recent facelift, the area below the station, the North Laine, with its own blend of retro anything, clothing, food, gifts (many of them esoteric, to put it politely), household bits and pieces, books and toys, is just as exciting. Don't ignore St James's Street (map F5), leading to Kemp Town, where there are more independent shops, and pedestrianized George Street in Hove with its many varied shops and restaurants and an altogether calmer feel.

Topolino Duo (page 75)

Shi-Shi (page 58)

TASTE THE DELIGHTS

You could eat out every day for a year in Brighton and Hove, and never have the same menu twice. Café culture has hit the city in a big way and there are many eating establishments that are open all day serving coffees, juices, smoothies, salads, cooked meals or simply tea and cakes. Vegetarian is big here and there are lots of good restaurants catering for non-meat eaters, including two top-class ones (see pages 77–78). It's perfectly possible to enjoy a morning or an afternoon with coffee and newspapers, with perhaps a plate of olives or tapas or a slice of pizza, and watch the whole hedonistic world go by.

SEE THE SEA LIFE

Take a walk on the underwater-side through the long tunnel at the Brighton Sea Life Centre on Marine Parade (map F5) and watch sharks, giant turtles and huge rays lazily swim by. Here you can pit your wits against an octopus and get close to crabs and brightly coloured sea anemones in the rock pool. Not too far away, on the other side of Brighton Pier, is the Fishing Museum (map D6), taking you right back to the days when 'Brighthelmstone' was a small fishing village, reliant mainly on the harvest of the seas for its livelihood. Even now that it's a cosmopolitan city by the sea, Brighton hasn't forgotten its fishing legacy. Fishermen still operate from here and you can buy fresh and smoked fish from the shop on the beach and watch nets being mended and spread out along the shingle to dry.

ENJOY THE ART

The Artists' Quarter on the seafront between the two piers consists of beach-level studios built into the arches. There's a huge variety of work and you can buy direct from the artists.

Back in town you can gain free entry to Brighton Museum and Art Gallery (map E4) where there is not only a good picture collection but also a fascinating permanent exhibition of 20th-century furniture and a lively look at the rise of Brighton from seaweed-strewn fishing village to the south coast's favourite playground. The redeveloped Museum and Art Gallery in Hove is another real pleasure with its toy gallery (spot the sleeping wizard), fine art collection and interesting film gallery, where you can see the development of film from its origins in magic lanterns, and other optical toys.

Sea Life Centre

Open: Brighton Museum and Art Gallery: Tue 10.00–19.00, Wed–Sat 10.00–17.00, Sun 14.00–17.00. Closed Mon (except bank holidays)

Hove Museum and Art Gallery: Tue–Sat 10.00–17.00, Sun 14.00–17.00

Entry: (both museums) free

Further information: pages 37 and 41

Open: Brighton Sea Life Centre: daily from 10.00 (last admission times vary)

Entry: under £10 (all day admission)

Open: Brighton Fishing Museum: daily; Mar–Nov: 10.00–17.00; Dec–Feb: 11.00–15.00

Entry: free

Further information: pages 39 and 35

Volks Electric Railway

TAKE THE TRAIN AND WALK WITH THE STARS

A chug along 2 kilometres (just over a mile) of seafront in the little carriages pulled by the trains of Volks Electric Railway (map F6) is a real pleasure. You're almost at the Marina when you reach the end of the line, so, while you're there, you can enjoy the Hollywood-style 'Walk of Fame', where you follow a trail detailing the names of the rich and famous associated with the city. Pick up a leaflet and follow the plaques set into the sidewalk to see how many stars love the city by the sea.

Open: Volks Electric Railway: Easter–mid Sep: Mon–Fri 11.00–17.00, Sat–Sun 11.00–18.00
Walk of Fame: daily from 10.00
Entry: Volks Electric Railway: fare under £3

Walk of Fame: free
Further information: page 48

PUT A PENNY IN THE SLOT

… and what will you see? Mechanical Memories (map D6) is the name of the Museum of Penny Slot Machines, situated in King's Road Arches on the seafront. Here for a small fee you can 'hire' a handful of old pennies and taste the old-fashioned delights of seaside entertainment before the age of electronic video games.

Open: Easter–Sep: 11.00–18.00 during school holidays and at weekends; during fine weekends in winter
Entry: free; small charge for using machines
Further information: page 42

GO TO CHURCH

Brighton has two Grade I listed churches, both extraordinary in their own way. St Bartholomew's in Ann Street (map E1) has the tallest nave in the country. The huge interior is dominated by a large chalk cross on the north wall. The Victorian St Michael and All Angels in Victoria Road (map A3) is a fusion of two churches containing the most lovely Arts and Crafts windows by William Morris, Ford Maddox Brown, Philip Webb and Edward Burne-Jones.

Open: for visitors: St Bartholomew's: Mon–Sat 9.30–13.00 and 14.00–16.30; St Michael and All Angels: Wed 15.30–17.30, Thu 12.30–14.30, Fri 15.30–17.30, Sat 9.30–11.30
Entry: (both churches) free
Further information: page 47

GOTHIC REVIVAL

St Peter's, in York Place, marks a change in Brighton's architectural style. At the end of the 19th century there was a move away from the light classical Regency style towards what was seen as the more moral and serious Gothic revival. Architect Sir Charles Barry, who also designed the Houses of Parliament, was at the forefront of this movement. St Peter's, which was designed by him in 1824 and built of white Portland stone, was one of the first churches to be built in this style in England.

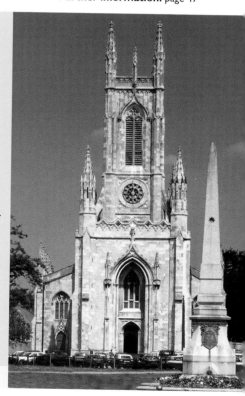

St Peter's Church

DOCTOR BRIGHTON

'Nobody goes abroad any more. Everybody is at Brighton,' wrote novelist and social commentator William Makepeace Thackeray in 1847. And so they were. 'Dr Brighton', as Thackeray dubbed the town, has worked its special magic for generations.

HOLIDAY IN BRIGHTON

'They came in by train from Victoria every five minutes, rocked down Queen's Road standing on the tops of the little local trams, stepped off in bewildered multitudes into fresh and glittering air: the new silver paint sparkled on the piers, the cream houses ran away into the west like a pale Victorian water-colour.' So wrote Graham Greene on the opening page of his classic *Brighton Rock,* describing the Whitsun holiday crowds invading Brighton in 1938.

Just 100 years earlier, in 1750, Dr Richard Russell had published his revolutionary cure-all based on the therapeutic properties of salt water: 'The sea washes away all the ills of mankind,' he declared. The 21-year-old Prince of Wales, later the Prince Regent, certainly thought so. He 'escaped' to Brighton to revel in the free and easy atmosphere, and where he went the rich and fashionable followed.

And did they enjoy themselves! Sea bathing, parties, gambling, extravagant dining, liaisons of all sorts, licit and illicit, were the order of the day. Brighton, no longer earning its keep from fishing and farming, saw a building boom, an explosion of service industries and an influx of wealth that rubbed off on everyone. The lovely Regency buildings in Brighton and Hove date from this sudden expansion.

Morning Promenade upon the Cliffs, Brighton, 1806

Brighton Pier

Banqueting Room, The Royal Pavilion

The culmination of the Georgian feel-good factor was the extraordinary Pavilion, built for the Prince Regent and finally completed in 1823.

By this time there was no going back. The railway arrived early in Victoria's reign and Brighton suddenly became everybody's favourite playground as new hotels were built and visitor attractions, such as the Aquarium and Volks Electric Railway, appeared on the seafront. The now derelict West Pier and, later, Brighton Pier were the main draw for thousands. Between the wars Brighton's popularity reached new heights. Dance halls, cinemas, an ice rink and spacious new parks were designed. Day-trippers and holidaymakers travelled on the new electric trams and thought of nothing but enjoying themselves.

Brighton's fortunes have waxed and waned, but today it's once more the centre of the universe for most of its inhabitants and millions of visitors, who recognize that the city is one of those rare places where you can drop all pretence and be yourself. There's an extraordinary cosmopolitan feel about the place, with its thriving gay community, bringing a special brand of art and culture, the night owls who like nothing better than to dance until dawn, and visitors who want to shop, eat and enjoy some time by the seaside.

Hove Beach

PLANNING YOUR VISIT

You might want to plunge straight away into The Lanes or rush to buy candyfloss on the pier, but if you take a little time to plan your visit you can make the most of Brighton. In a city where every attraction seems to shout 'look at me' it's easy to get distracted.

The glorious Regency Pavilion is a must-see and you can't possibly visit Brighton without a walk to the end of the pier. On the face of it these two historic constructions couldn't be more different, but each was built with the promise of pleasure in mind.

The Royal Pavilion

THE FIRST DAY

In its heyday the Prince Regent's gorgeous Eastern palace by the sea was one of the marvels of the modern world, and so it is today. Stand back to enjoy the extraordinary domed and turreted stucco exterior before going inside. Join a guided tour or buy a guidebook and wander round at your own pace. Now that the Pavilion has been restored and some of the original furniture, on loan from HM The Queen, is back in place the effect is sumptuous. Visitors gasp as they enter the Banqueting Room, its long table lavishly set for a dessert course, illuminated by the light-breathing dragons in the great chandelier. The Music Room has the same effect, with elaborate lotus-blossom chandeliers, rich red, blue and gold draped curtains supported by silver dragons and Chinese scenes painted on the walls. Throughout the building there is more of the same, and you'll need a couple of hours to have a good look at everything, including Rex Whistler's mildly naughty painting of the Prince Regent awakening the spirit of Brighton.

Dodgems on Brighton Pier

TREAT YOURSELF
Go on – forget you're a grown-up with a responsible job and an image – just walk onto the pier and enjoy your-self. Play the fairground games, try the rides, have a gamble, buy candyfloss (you don't have to eat it but the photographs look good), breathe in quantities of sea air and flop in a deckchair to watch an often weird and wonderful world go by.

Time for coffee now – wander across to The Lanes for refreshment and a good browse before finding lunch at a pub, restaurant or café. You'll find yourself spoilt for choice but many visitors make a beeline for East Street where there are cheerful Italian restaurants and the highly acclaimed vegetarian Terre à Terre. Food For Friends in Prince Albert Street is another vegetarian eatery enjoyed by carnivores as well.

Now for some bracing sea breezes. Head for the front and Brighton Pier. This is the epitome of the British seaside – fish and chips, fortune-tellers, the Dolphin Derby, candyfloss and amuse-ment arcades, fairground rides and stripy deckchairs to collapse into. You can snack on jellied eels and cockles or fish and chips, or simply enjoy a stroll to the end of the pier and back, watching the world enjoying itself.

If clubbing's your scene, look no farther than King's Road Arches at beach level, where you'll find some of Brighton's favourites, including the Funky Buddha Lounge, Honey Club, The Beach, Zap and Arc.

Kiosk selling shellfish

THE NEXT DAY OR TWO

If you managed to squeeze all that into one day, don't worry. Brighton has plenty more to keep you busy. Here are some 'add-on' suggestions to choose from to make the most of your stay.

Tread the streets

Follow one of our walks on pages 26–31, or join one of the Blue Badge guides who offer walking tours in the city – details from the Brighton Visitor Information Centre in Bartholomew Square (see page 94). Another series of

Brighton walks are led by Blue Badge guide Glenda Clarke and her colleagues. Themed walks include a 'Quadrophenia' (remember the film?) tour, a Ghost Walk, Legends of the Lanes, and Murders and Mystery. Details are on page 94.

Take the bus or the train

Open-top bus tours of the city last for around an hour, during which time you'll get a full commentary about what you are seeing. The buses leave from Brighton Pier (see page 83). You won't learn much about Brighton during the 2-kilometre (1.25-mile) ride on Volks Electric Railway (by the pier) but you'll enjoy a chug along the seafront. The little train stops near the Marina and the nudist beach (see page 10).

The Marina

Sit on the beach

There's plenty of beach for everyone, although the area between the two piers is where you'll see most of the action. This part is served by cafés, restaurants, paddling pools and carousel rides for children, and a civilized boardwalk to protect your feet from the shingle. The main beaches have lifeguards who will advise on sea conditions for swimming.

S AFE BATHING
Pool Valley (map E5), where today you will find the bus and coach station, was once an area of Brighton given over to the fashion for bathing. John Awsiter, a doctor, established hot and cold saltwater baths here in 1769.

A fishy story

Brighton Sea Life Centre (see page 39) is well laid out and enjoyable. There's a long underwater tunnel, giant turtles, huge shoals of colourful tropical fish and a rock pool where you can tickle the crabs. Built in the best Victorian tradition, the architecture is pretty amazing too. Not far away from the Sea Life Centre is the Fishing Museum (see page 35), where you can explore catches of the past, and also buy fresh fish for supper from the men who go down to the sea in boats today.

Specs (page 59)

THE NORTH LAINE

There are Lanes and Laines in Brighton and it doesn't do to get them confused. The North Laine, the area between North Street and Trafalgar Street, is a maze of narrow, criss-crossing streets, some crammed with an eclectic mix of shops. The word 'laine' used to be the local term for a field, which is what this part of town was in the late 17th century.

THE LANES

These winding, narrow alley-ways, which now house many of Brighton's famous jewellery and antique shops, were once the shady side of town, where smugglers hid and French raiders engaged in running battles with the inhabitants. They are just off the seafront and are a Brighton institution.

Explore the shops

True shoppers won't be satisfied with a brief visit to The Lanes. You can easily spend the best part of a day here before moving up to the North Laine area (map D2/3–E2/3) where tiny streets, some pedestrian-only, contain the most exuberant and extraordinary collection of shops you'll find anywhere. Don't miss Trafalgar Street, underneath the station arches (map D2/E2). The shops in Kemp Town are quite different – look for St James's Street, leading off the Old Steine. The Marina, farther to the east, is a complete shopping village in itself. This is where you'll find outlets selling designer goods at low prices. There's contrast again in the centre of Hove on the western side of Brighton. Visit pedestrianized George Street, for a wide variety of shops.

Absorb the history

Both Brighton and Hove museums

Brunswick Terrace, Hove

(see pages 37 and 41) have excellent local history displays and you can learn a lot in a most enjoyable way about 'Dr Brighton' and the area's transformation from fishing village to holiday playground. A walk around the Brunswick Square area in Hove and a visit to the restored Regency Town House there will explain much about the development of Regency Brighton and Hove. If you're on the other side of town, enjoy the splendid Regency buildings in Kemp Town, as far as Sussex Square and Lewes Crescent.

Pack up a picnic

There is no shortage of beach to sit on and what could be nicer on a sunny day than a picnic to enjoy after your paddle? Cheat a little and buy excellent deli food from Bona Foodie or the Cherry Tree Deli in St James's Street (map F5) or from The Lanes Deli and Pasta Shop in Meeting House Lane (map D4). If you'd rather be surrounded by greenery, turn to pages 50–51 to find a park or garden for your picnic. Or simply buy good old fish and chips or a plate of shellfish on the pier, bag a deckchair – and enjoy your meal.

WALKS

There are excellent guided walks available in Brighton (see page 83) but you might like to go it alone. This section suggests three routes, allowing you to see much of the picturesque old town, the seafront and the historic area around the Royal Pavilion.

TWITTENS, CATCREEPS AND SHOPS WALK

'Twitten' is a local word describing a narrow lane, while a 'catcreep' is a flight of steps connecting two paths at different levels, on a hill. This walk, which incidentally takes you through some of Brighton's best shopping streets, uses lots of these narrow lanes.

Start in Trafalgar Street, 'underneath the arches' below Brighton Station. Walk down the hill, stopping perhaps at the Toy and Model Museum (see page 40), to Sydney Street. Turn right down this bustling little street and right again into Gloucester Road. You might like to continue to the right to explore the

street before retracing your steps to Kensington Gardens on your left. This is at the heart of the North Laine, the name of this area. At the bottom of Kensington Gardens, cross North Road into Gardner Street, then cross

Church Street and walk down Bond Street.

You are now out of the North Laine area and, once across busy North Street, into the famous Lanes. To the left you'll see Meeting House Lane,

Kensington Gardens

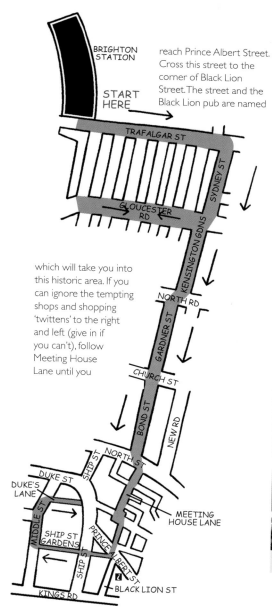

BRIGHTON STATION

START HERE

TRAFALGAR ST

GLOUCESTER RD

SYDNEY ST

KENSINGTON GDNS

NORTH RD

GARDNER ST

CHURCH ST

BOND ST

NEW RD

NORTH ST

DUKE ST

SHIP ST

DUKE'S LANE

MIDDLE ST

SHIP ST GARDENS

PRINCE ALBERT ST

SHIP ST

MEETING HOUSE LANE

KINGS RD

BLACK LION ST

reach Prince Albert Street. Cross this street to the corner of Black Lion Street. The street and the Black Lion pub are named

which will take you into this historic area. If you can ignore the tempting shops and shopping 'twittens' to the right and left (give in if you can't), follow Meeting House Lane until you

for the Flemish refugees who settled here 500 years ago and whose emblem was a black lion. On the wall of the pub there is a plaque to Deryk Carver, who was burned for his Protestant faith in 1555.

Take this little street on your right to cross Ship Street and then squeeze down another twitten, narrow Ship Street Gardens, ahead of you. Turn right into Middle Street and you'll spot a blue plaque on the wall of No. 20b to William Friese Green, the father of cinematography. On your right, past the Mecca Bingo Club (once an ice rink), you'll see Duke's Lane. Turn down here and you're back in Ship Street and Prince Albert Street with the Visitor Information Centre just down the road in St Bartholomew Square.

Mecca Bingo Club

BESIDE THE SEA WALK

This walk begins in the heart of the old city and makes its way to the seafront to the beach and pier. Although the fishermen don't hang their nets out to dry on the Old Steine any more, that's what they used to do, when it was a large open, stony place ('steine' is a Saxon word meaning 'stony'). Now it's a green and grassy area around which the traffic rushes.

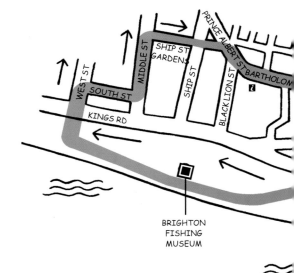

BRIGHTON
FISHING
MUSEUM

Start at Old Steine and head for St James's Street, which is the western end of fashionable Kemp Town. There is as good a mix of shops and restaurants here and, as you walk up the hill, you'll catch glimpses of the sea down the narrow streets on your right.

When you reach Rock Place or Lower Rock Gardens on your right, turn down towards the sea. You'll find yourself at Marine Parade with its shops and cafés. Cross the road to the seafront – and Volks Electric Railway. If you fancy a ride up to the Marina and back, hop on.

It will be a pleasant diversion. Once back at the terminal, you're just a step away from Brighton Pier with its games, gambling, bars, restaurant, funfair, shops, entertainment and deckchairs. It won't cost you a penny to walk on. Half of you should take the opportunity to visit the Ladies loo with its wonderfully ornate Victorian tiles.

Once you've exhausted these traditional delights, look for steps descending

to the beach and have a stroll along the boardwalk between the two piers. You can admire the art on display in the 'arches', visit the Fishing Museum, have a fairground ride on the 'Gallopers', or simply sit and gaze out to sea for a while. Continue your stroll

The boardwalk

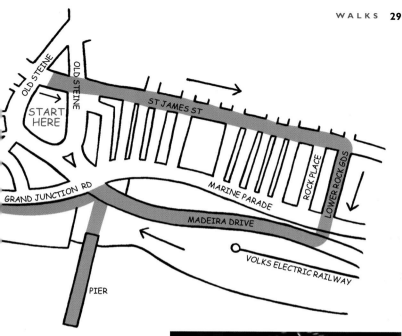

until you reach a pedestrian underpass tunnelling beneath busy King's Road. Cross here and turn right into South Street. At the end turn left into Middle Street, right again down narrow Ship Street Gardens, then cross Ship Street into Prince Albert Street and Bartholomews. Turn left into the pedestrianized part of East Street, which widens into a square full of café tables where you can sit, eat and drink and listen to the street musicians.

The 'Gallopers'

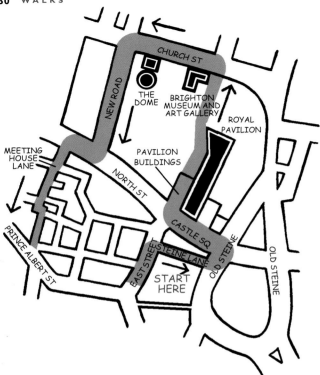

CHURCH ST

NEW ROAD

THE
DOME

BRIGHTON
MUSEUM AND
ART GALLERY

ROYAL
PAVILION

MEETING
HOUSE
LANE

PAVILION
BUILDINGS

NORTH ST

CASTLE SQ

OLD STEINE

OLD STEINE

PRINCE ALBERT ST

EAST STREET

STEINE LANE

START
HERE

A LIFELONG LOVE

King George IV, who was Prince Regent when he married the beautiful Catholic Maria Fitzherbert in secret, died at the age of 67. Despite the fact that he'd been forced to divorce her and marry his cousin Caroline of Brunswick and had numerous affairs, he apparently never really loved anyone but Maria. As he lay in his coffin he wore her portrait in a locket that was buried with him.

REGENCY WALK

This is only a short walk, but if you allow time for a visit to the Royal Pavilion, it will take the best part of a morning or afternoon. Throw in lunch and some shopping and you've made a day of it. Start near Al Forno restaurant in the pedestrianized part of East Street in The Lanes. This Brighton favourite was once the home of Martha Gunn, the most famous of the women 'dippers' – those who helped early sea bathers in and out of the water.

Opposite you'll see a passageway called Steine Lane. Follow this short twitten (narrow lane) and at the end, on the right, you'll see Steine House, now the YMCA, but once the home of Maria Fitzherbert, the secret wife of the Prince Regent and said to be his only true love. Lord Henry Barrymore once rode his horse up the staircase here. The Prince installed the beautiful 'Mrs Prince' in Steine House to be near him in the Royal Pavilion. Turn left and left again into Castle Square, cross North Street into Pavilion Buildings and go through the Indian Gateway into the Pavilion Gardens. At this point you might like to visit the Pavilion – it is one of the great buildings of Britain, unforgettable in its architecture and furnishing. The Gardens themselves are pleasant, while the Museum in the northeast corner is worth a visit too. As you walk through the Gardens you'll see the great Dome – now a concert hall but built to house the horses and indoor riding school for the Prince Regent.

Leave by the North Gate – you'll see a statue of the man himself, when he became George IV, on the right. Turn left up Church Street and left again down New Road, built to stop the nosy people of Brighton from peering into the royal windows. You'll pass the Theatre Royal, nearly 200 years old and still a favourite venue with the play-going public. Cross North Street and turn right. You'll soon see Meeting House Lane, taking you back into The Lanes where you'll find coffee, lunch and plenty of retail therapy.

The Dome Theatre

SIGHTSEEING

Of course you'll want to make the most of the sea air, walk out to the end of the pier, enjoy the best shopping for miles around and gasp at the splendours of the Royal Pavilion. But Brighton and Hove have a lot more as well to make your stay varied and special.

TAKING A DIP

The rush to Brighton to take a fashionable and healthy dip in the invigorating waters led to all sorts of employment opportunities. 'Dippers' – men and women employed to aid bathers – did very well, giving swimming lessons and generally helping people in and out of the horse-drawn bathing machines that took them right into the sea. Chief among these dippers was the famous Martha Gunn who, like many Brighton notables, is buried in St Nicholas graveyard in Dyke Road.

Barlow Collection of Chinese Art
University of Sussex, Falmer

If you are interested in Chinese Art, especially Tang and Song ceramics, it is worth visiting this outstanding collection held in the University Library. More than 450 objects, mainly ceramics, bronzes and jades, spanning three millennia of Chinese history, were collected by distinguished civil servant Sir Alan Barlow before his death in 1968. The collection was bequeathed to the University of Sussex to be used for teaching and display purposes.

Open: Tue and Thu 11.30–14.30; group visits can be arranged at other times
Entry: free (a donation is welcomed)
Tel: 01273 678199
Website: www.sussex.ac.uk/arthistory or www.24hourmuseum.org.uk
Disabled access: full

Booth Museum of Natural History
Dyke Road

The stuffed birds, collected by the naturalist who gave his name to the museum, form the core of this collection. Then there are tens of thousands of insects, including beetles and many beautiful butterflies. For those who like their nature big, there's the skeleton of a killer whale and an assortment of dinosaur bones. Children will enjoy the interactive section.

Open: Mon–Wed, Fri–Sat 10.00–17.00; Sun 14.00–17.00; (opening hours may be restricted Oct–Mar). Closed Thu
Entry: free
Tel: 01273 292777
Website: www.booth.virtualmuseum.info
Disabled access: full
Other facilities: shop

SOLDIER AND FISHWIFE

Among the headstones in St Nicholas graveyard is that of Phoebe Hassel, a remarkable woman who spent 17 years disguised as a man. Phoebe fell in love with soldier Samuel Golding. When he was sent to the West Indies in 1728, she enlisted in the army and lived as a soldier, undetected until Golding was invalided out, when they at last married. At his death she remarried and sold fish from a barrow in Brighton. She lived to be 108.

Booth Museum of Natural History

Brighton beach

Don't be disappointed to find a neat shingle beach rather than sand. There's 11 kilometres (7 miles) of it, which is just as well, because as soon as the sun emerges so do people in their hundreds, intent on a quick tan, a doze in a deckchair and perhaps a dip in the sea. Because of the steep slope of the shingle down to the sea, people sitting on the famous pebbles are silhouetted against the sea and the sky and you get a strange sense of déjà vu as that image, beloved of newspaper picture editors everywhere, imprints itself on your consciousness again and again as you walk along the front.

If you like your beach well served with bars, cafés, paddling pools, children's play-ground, games and even a timbered boardwalk to save your feet from the pebbles, choose the area between the two piers. You're only a step or two away from an evening's clubbing as some of the coolest venues in town are situated in the restored Victorian King's Road Arches, stretching down to the sea. Here is where you'll find the Artists' Quarter, where you can buy paintings and other artwork direct from the studios.

Walk beyond the West Pier towards Hove and you'll notice the esplanade turning into stretches of manicured lawns. When you come to the Peace Statue, you've reached the official start of well-mannered Hove.

Walk the other way, or hop onto Volks Electric Railway (see page 48), and just before you reach the Marina you'll notice that the shingle is built up on three sides to make a neat wall, with the open side facing the sea. This is to protect your sensibilities from those who sunbathe in the nude. But if you like an all-over tan, that's the place to go.

Brighton beach

Peace Statue

Brighton Fishing Museum

Arch 201, King's Road Arches; map D6

There's a lot of nostalgia in this museum set among the arches, which are still used by working fishermen (you'll see their nets spread on the beach) as they have been since 1860. The museum deals with the fishing industry in general and that of Brighton in particular. The centrepiece is a lovely old, full-size Sussex clinker-built beach fishing boat.

You can buy fresh fish and shellfish from the stalls and also fish smoked in the traditional way. If you're there during the Brighton Festival in May (see page 84), you'll see the Blessing of the Nets ritual and perhaps enjoy the barbecued mackerel that goes with it.

Open: daily; Mar–Nov: 10.00–17.00; Dec–Feb: 11.00–15.00
Entry: free
Tel: 01273 723064
Website: www.visitbrighton.com
Disabled access: partial
Other facilities: shop; boat trips on the *Skylark* from the beach below the arch during summer

Brighton Fishing Museum

Brighton Marina

Brighton Marina

2 km (1.2 miles) east of city centre

If you want a day's shopping for bargains, this is the place to go with dozens of famous chain stores offering discounts off high-street prices. There are many restaurants, bars and cafés too. Entertainment includes a casino, a multiplex cinema and a leisure centre. This is where you can charter fishing boats or take an evening trip on the water. Oh – and you can moor your own boat here, too.

Open: shopping centre: daily; 10.00–18.00; bars, restaurants and leisure activities: 10.00–late

Tel: 01273 818504

Website: www.brightonmarinauk.co.uk

Disabled access: full

Other facilities: free parking

STILL IN FULL SAIL

One of Brighton's most famous and oldest hotels, and one with many literary connections, is the four-star Old Ship, on the seafront. Thackeray wrote much of *Vanity Fair* while staying here and sent his two main characters, George and Amelia, to Brighton for their honeymoon. Charles Dickens, another Brighton fan, stayed here, while Graham Greene makes his *Brighton Rock* protagonist, Hale, invite the luscious Ida Arnold to lunch at the Old Ship. Sadly for him she declined.

Brighton Museum and Art Gallery
Royal Pavilion Gardens; map E4

This beautifully laid-out series of galleries has had a £10-million facelift – and it shows. There's a wonderful permanent exhibition of 20th-century art and design, including furniture by makers such as Frank Gehry, and an equally interesting performance-themed show upstairs. There is also a gallery with some fine paintings by Ben Nicholson and one of Brighton beach by Wilson Steer.

Many visitors will enjoy 'exploring Brighton' and 'images of Brighton', showing in pictures, words and sound the transformation of Brighton from fishing village to fashionable town, to the venue for the 1964 bank holiday scuffles between mods and rockers.

DON'T MISS
The red Lambretta Lil 50 with its mock tiger-skin seat.

Open: Tue 10.00–19.00, Wed–Sat 10.00–17.00, Sun 14.00–17.00. Closed Mon (except bank holidays)
Entry: free

Brighton Museum and Art Gallery

BRIGHTON MUSEUM & ART GALLERY

Tel: 01273 290900
Website: www.virtualmuseum.info
Disabled access: full
Other facilities: shop and café

Brighton Pier

Brighton Sea Life Centre

Brighton Pier
Marine Parade; map E6

This is the real thing – vulgar, brash, exciting, beautiful and bracing all at once. Here you can eat candyfloss, fish and chips and jellied eels, have your fortune told and your handwriting analysed, win or lose on the gambling machines, slump in a deckchair, or scare yourself witless on the fairground rides.

Just over 100 years old and 525 metres (1,722 feet) long, the pier is a listed building with an attractive dome (housing the arcade) and filigree wrought iron-work. There's no charge to wander onto it, sit down in a deckchair, or take a bracing turn to the end and back.
Open: daily (weather permitting); summer: 9.00–2.00; winter: 10.00–21.30
Entry: free (there is a charge for amusements and rides)
Tel: 01273 609361
Website: www.brightonpier.co.uk
Disabled access: full

Brighton Sea Life Centre
Marine Parade; map F5

This claims to be the world's oldest aquarium; it's certainly one of the most interesting with an underwater tunnel taking you past sharks, giant rays and turtles. There are shoals of brightly coloured tropical fish and, best of all, the octopuses, whose intelligence is put to the test in a series of (food-rewarding) challenges. At certain times during the day you can go to the 'touch pool' to commune with crabs and get acquainted with anemones. All in all it's an enlightening and enlivening experience in an updated original Victorian building.

DON'T MISS

The octopuses – one, a Giant Pacific, measures 4.6 metres (15 feet) across.
Open: daily from 10.00 (last admission times vary)
Entry: under £10 (all day admission)
Tel: 01273 604234
Website: www.sealifeeurope.com
Disabled access: limited
Other facilities: café, gift shop and soft play area

Brighton Toy and Model Museum
Trafalgar Street; map D2

Tucked away beneath the arches of
Brighton Railway Station is a playtime
paradise, a world-class toy museum with
more than 10,000 toys and models on
display. Every boy and his dad will make
a beeline for the model train collection,
while there are plenty of other toys
(including a superb gathering of tin-plate
toys) to keep everyone in the family
happy. You'll see soldiers, aeroplanes,
dolls, teddy bears, buses and ships.
On some weekends they run the
splendid 0-gauge railway and it's hard
to know who enjoys it most – the
volunteers or the visitors.
Open: Tue–Fri 10.00–17.00,
Sat 11.00–17.00
Entry: under £5
Tel: 01273 749494
Website: www.
brightontoymuseum.co.uk
Disabled access: limited
Other facilities: shop

British Engineerium Museum of Steam and Mechanical Antiquities
Nevill Road, Hove

If you're into engines you'll probably
want to spend your whole holiday here,
among the gleaming and sometimes hiss-
ing and steaming monsters powered by
hot air and steam. The whole collection
is shown off in a restored Victorian
pumping station and, on the first Sunday
in the month, steam's up. Children will
enjoy the interactive Giant's Toolbox
while motorcycle enthusiasts will find
plenty to drool over, too.
Open: daily; 10.00–17.00

Entry: under £5
Tel: 01273 559583
Website: www.
britishengineerium.com
Disabled access: limited

British Engineerium Museum of Steam
and Mechanical Antiquities

Hove Museum and Art Gallery

Hove Museum and Art Gallery
19 New Church Road, Hove

Set in an Italianate Victorian villa, built in the same style as Queen Victoria's Osborne House, this newly refurbished museum is a firm favourite with visitors and locals alike. Young people enjoy the Toy Gallery with its snoring wizard and under-floor trains. Two galleries display contemporary craft, introduce 20th-century craft pioneers and show-case special objects from the regional crafts collection. Local history is explored; there's a fascinating look at the development of film as well as a fine art exhibition space.

Open: Tue–Sat 10.00–17.00, Sun 14.00–17.00
Entry: free
Tel: 01273 290200
Website: www.virtualmuseum.info
Disabled access: full
Other facilities: shop and café

Kemp Town
map F5 and eastwards

Brighton is full of interesting enclaves and this area, stretching from the Old Steine (map E5) along St James's Street as far as the Marina, and down to the seafront, is one of them. Here the shops are again interesting and different, with good restaurants and upmarket antiques, flowers and furnishings on display. Things simmer down a bit once you get to Kemp Town proper, around St George's Road, and become very sedate around Sussex Square and Lewes Crescent.

The Lanes
map D5

Not to be confused with the North Laine (see page 42), these winding, twisting shop-crammed streets are the reason many visitors come back to

Brighton time and time again. You can lose yourself in a narrow passageway, peering in windows to look at jewellery, antiques, books, old stamps, shoes or china – and suddenly emerge into a light and modern square, before plunging back into the ever-fascinating exploration of these tiny streets. Here, and in North Laine, the very narrow passages are locally known as 'twittens', a Sussex word used for a constricted path that connects wider streets. If your twitten has steps in it, it's known as a 'catcreep'. You could spend a whole day in this area, sitting outside and drinking coffee or eating lunch, making slow progress round the hundreds of shops, or trying out one or two of the pubs. The atmosphere is happy – everyone likes The Lanes.

Mechanical Memories – the Museum of Penny Slot Machines
King's Road Arches; map D6

Put a penny in the slot – and wait to see what happens. 'Old-fashioned fun at old-fashioned prices' is the slogan here and, for those who don't remember the delights of one-time seaside entertainment, it's an eye-opener and a joy. This Museum is part of the National Slot Machine collection and has a huge variety of non-electric automatic entertainments dating from the 1890s.

Open: Easter–Sep: 11.00–18.00 during school holidays and weekends; during fine weekends in winter

Entry: free; small charge for using machines – old pennies provided

Tel: 01273 608620

Disabled access: full

North Laine

North Laine
map D2/3–E2/3

This is an area of tiny streets, some purely residential, some crammed with the wackiest shops you're likely to find anywhere. It's an old-established area, developed nearly 250 years ago to house workers between Trafalgar Street and North Street. Before that, the area was an arable field, known as a 'laine'. Now it is full of life. Early in the morning the many cafés, coffee shops and breakfast bars are buzzing, and it stays that way all day. You'll find bead shops, kite shops, therapists, shops full of retro clothing and furniture, old-fashioned tobacconists, book stores, market stalls, hippie-dippie clothing, even a café selling 'soyachinos' (coffee made with soya milk). See pages 52–68 for a more complete guide to the shops. You can easily spend a morning exploring this bustling network and then stay on for lunch.

Drawing Room, Preston Manor

Preston Manor
Preston Drove

More than 20 rooms are on view in this restored Edwardian country house. You can see both upstairs and downstairs, from the day nursery on the upper floor to the servants' quarters down below. There are collections of furniture, silver, paintings, family memorabilia – and 124 Buddhist Chinese lions. The house was occupied by the wealthy Stanfords, who developed parts of Hove and lived in splendour just outside. But a family feud meant that the fortunes of the Stanfords were dissipated and the house became the property of Brighton and Hove Council in 1932. The house is surrounded by a 24-hectare (60-acre) park with walled garden (see page 51).

Open: daily; Mon 13.00–17.00, Tue–Sat 10.00–17.00, Sun 14.00–17.00 (opening hours may be restricted between Oct–Mar)

Entry: under £5
Tel: 01273 290900
Website: www.virtualmuseum.info
Disabled access: none to house; full to park

Regency Town House
Brunswick Square, Hove

When the craze for sea-bathing took off, Brighton and Hove became the place to be seen. The advent of the Prince Regent made it even more fashionable and a building boom ensued, nowhere more elegantly than in Hove's Brunswick Square. Lillie Langtry, Edwardian actress and mistress to the king, certainly thought so – she lived there. Now the so-called 'Regency Town House' at No. 13 is undergoing careful restoration. There is still some way to go but enough has been completed to allow an interesting hour-long tour, which you must book beforehand.

Regency Town House

Open: all year; until restoration is complete, tours must be booked – please telephone the number below
Entry: under £5
Tel: 01273 206306
Website: www.rth.org.uk
Disabled access: none

The Royal Pavilion
Pavilion Parade; map E4

When the 21-year-old George, Prince of Wales, escaped from the stifling atmosphere of court to stay in Brighton with his disreputable uncle the Duke of Cumberland, he thought he had discovered heaven. He came back for more, secretly married his Catholic mistress Maria Fitzherbert and set her up in a villa, renting a respectable farmhouse for himself nearby. In 1787 the farmhouse was transformed into a neoclassical 'marine pavilion' by architect Henry Holland. It was soon to be dwarfed by the magnificent domed building nearby, designed to house the Prince's 60 horses in some comfort. As George (known fondly by his nearest and dearest as 'Prinny') became first Prince Regent (1811) and then King George IV (1820),

Brighton's status as a small fishing town changed to that of a highly fashionable resort. The marine pavilion, too, was transformed into the extraordinary domed and turreted palace that we see today.

Architect John Nash, with the prince at his elbow, drew up plans for this oriental fantasy in 1815 when building started. Two of the most fashionable interior decorators of the day, Frederick Crace and Robert Jones, outdid each other with their designs, producing a fantastical series of rooms, all Eastern in style; dragons breathe fire from chandeliers and curtain poles, bamboo patterns enliven the walls, lotus blossoms provide illumination, and serpents are twined in improbable places. Everything is sumptuous and everywhere there are mirrors, so that the whole place feels twice as large. Even the kitchens are embellished with pillars designed to look like tall palm trees. Upstairs the bedrooms are in the Chinese style – reds and golds, lacquer work, dragons and bamboo.

South Gallery

Banqueting Room

Although the Pavilion can only be described in superlatives, a sense of fun prevails. In fact once the Prince Regent became king, he barely used the Royal Pavilion after its completion in 1823. It was used as a royal residence by William IV and in a desultory fashion by Queen Victoria, who, much preferring Osborne House on the Isle of Wight, sold it to the town of Brighton in 1850. It must have been a sad and neglected

sight, stripped of furniture, wallpaper, chimneypieces, decorations and fixtures. But the restoration has been superb and once more you can marvel at the craft, the workmanship and the sheer sumptuousness of it all.

DON'T MISS
The Banqueting Room with its incredible dragon-held central chandelier. This weighs exactly one ton and the light appears to come from the fiery breath of six smaller dragons, breathing flame into lotus petals. The room was designed by Robert Jones.
The Music Room, where Frederick Crace carried on Jones' dragon and lotus theme. Carved silvered and gilded dragons support the massively draped curtains, while the decorated oval opaque glass panels in the ceiling were designed to be backlit at night. Magnificent lotus bowls hang from the ceiling to light the room.
The South Galleries upstairs, with their vivid blue walls enlivened by imitation bamboo and their splendid, painted glass windows in the ceiling (called lay lights).
The Great Kitchen with its high ceiling supported by cast-iron columns designed to resemble palm trees.
Open: daily; Apr–Sep: 9.30–17.45 (last admission 17.00); Oct–Mar: 10.00–17.15 (last admission 16.30). Closed 25 and 26 Dec. Guided tours (extra charge) at 11.30 and 14.30 daily
Entry: under £10
Tel: 01273 290900
Website: www.royalpavilion.org.uk
Disabled access: limited
Other facilities: café and shop

St Bartholomew's Church
Ann Street; map E1

This extraordinary church, which has the
tallest nave in the country and a huge
rose window, is, like St Michael's (see
below), a Grade 1 listed building. When
it was built in 1872 it was vilified as an
'excrescence' and a 'cheese warehouse',
but you cannot deny its awe-inspiring
beauty. Inside it seems vast and a huge,
hand-carved chalk cross dominates the
north wall.

Open: for visitors: Mon–Sat
9.30–13.00 and 14.00–16.30
Entry: free
Tel: 01273 620491
Website: visitbrighton.com
Disabled access: full

St Michael and All Angels Church
Victoria Road; map A3

Here you have a church within a church,
the two making such a spectacular
whole that it is reckoned to be one of
the most outstanding in England. The old
church, built by Bodley in 1858 and with
beautiful Arts and Crafts windows by
William Morris, Ford Maddox Brown,
Edward Burne-Jones and Philip Webb, is
now the south aisle. Around it is William
Burges's great 'extension', which in reality
forms the body of the church. With its
enormous Victorian Gothic nave, marble
sanctuary and altar and wrought-iron
screens, St Michael's is an example of
Victorian church architecture at its best.
Visitors to the Brighton Festival, which
happens during May, will find many musi-
cal events staged here – the acoustics
are good. Mass is said daily in High
Church of England tradition.

Open: for visitors: Wed 15.30–17.30,
Thu 12.30–14.30, Fri 15.30–17.30, Sat
9.30–11.30
Entry: free
Tel: 01273 727362
Website: www.
saintmichaelsbrighton.org
Disabled access: limited

Sussex Square
near Brighton Marina

It's worth the walk along St James's
Street to Kemp Town to see Sussex
Square and Lewes Crescent and the
other graceful Regency buildings built
with care by architects Charles Augustus
Busby and the two Amon Wilds (father
and son) in the first flush of Brighton's
rise to popularity. In the communal
gardens is a 'secret' rose garden with a
tunnel leading to the beach, said to have
been the inspiration for one-time resident Lewis Carroll's 'tunnel' in *Through
the Looking-Glass*. You could walk back to
the city centre along the seafront or hop
onto Volks Electric Railway for the trip
back to town.

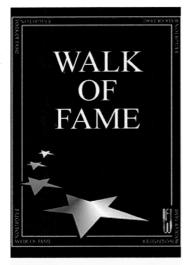

Walk of Fame

Volks Electric Seafront Railway
Madeira Drive; map F6

This is the most pleasant way to travel up to the Marina from Brighton Pier, chugging slowly along the seafront on Britain's oldest electric railway. The little train, starting off with a traditional toot, pulls open-sided carriages the 2 kilometres (1.25 miles), stopping briefly halfway. The trains run every 15 minutes and your return ticket is valid all day. Kids love it.

Open: Easter–mid Sep: Mon–Fri 11.00–17.00, Sat–Sun 11.00–18.00
Fare: under £3
Tel: 01273 292718
Website: www.brighton-hove.gov.uk
Disabled access: full

Walk of Fame
Brighton Marina

Just like its Hollywood forerunner, the Brighton Walk of Fame commemorates the many celebrities and distinguished men and women who have become connected with the city in one way or another. Plaques, video and books describe the celebs. The hundred-plus names range from Leo Sayer, Norman Wisdom, Steve Coogan and Zoe Ball to Julie Christie, The Who and Nigel Kennedy. As time goes on, the list just grows longer.

Open: daily from 10.00
Entry: free
Tel: 01273 672921; 01273 670701 for Walk of Fame guide
Website: www.walkoffame.co.uk
Disabled access: full

West Pier
Brighton Seafront; map A6

All you can do is gaze mournfully at this once lovely building, now literally falling in to the sea. Designed by Eugenious Birch and built in 1866, it became the first Grade 1 listed pier in England but was damaged in the Second World War. Although repairs were made, maintenance didn't keep up with the decay and the whole structure was closed to the public in 1975. Recent attempts to raise money to restore it have foundered, but the powers that be have not yet given up hope. Our loss has to be someone's gain – in this case a murmuration of thousands of starlings who roost there at night. It's become a ritual to gather on nearby Brighton Pier (see page 39) an hour before sunset to see the birds wheeling and diving against the sunset, before they finally settle down for the hours of darkness.

Open: no access
Tel: 01273 321499
Website: www.westpier.co.uk

END OF THE PIER?

Despite the fact that it is the only Grade I listed pier in the country, Brighton's West Pier seems to have no future. In its glory days stars such as Charlie Chaplin, Ellen Terry, Stan Laurel, Rex Harrison and Ralph Richardson performed in its theatre. The pier was closed because of its dilapidated state, and in 2002 and 2004 parts of it fell into the sea. Plans to restore it have come to nothing and it is estimated it would cost more than £30 million just to make it structurally sound.

West Pier

BREATHING
SPACE

TREAT YOURSELF

Every morning the charming attendants put out stacks of deckchairs in Royal Pavilion Gardens and, for a small fee, they're yours for the morning or the day. Take a good book, admire the astounding minarets of the most exotic building in Britain, or doze the day away.

Royal Pavilion Gardens

If it's fresh air you're after, all you need to do is to wander down to the seafront and sit on the beach for a while. There is also plenty of green space inland, where you can sit, stroll or picnic.

Royal Pavilion Gardens
map D4/E4
You can hire a deckchair or just sit on the grass in parts of the well-stocked garden surrounding the Royal Pavilion and the Museum. Don't be surprised if you are accosted by a friendly thrush – the garden is full of them.

St Ann's Well Gardens, Hove
Just where Brighton and Hove merge, this pretty park has a good children's playground, café, tennis courts and a bowling green. Squirrels chatter at you from the grass and there's a large ornamental fish pond and winding paths beneath mature trees. Another attractive feature is the thoughtfully planted scented garden.

Queen's Park
This lovely park, built as an ornamental garden nearly 200 years ago, has views down to the sea. If you're feeling energetic you can play tennis or, less energetic, bowls. There are plenty of trees for shade and picnicking families are welcome. A chunk of the countryside in the city, Queen's Park is home to foxes, hedgehogs, squirrels and bats, has wild and scented gardens and a winding stream. The children's playground is well laid out, while free entertainment is often laid on for youngsters during the busy summer months.

St Ann's Well Gardens

Hove Park
To the north of Hove, this is a large circular park with Victorian architecture and good family facilities – a café, children's playground and a miniature railway which is operated by volunteers on certain days. There are bowls in the summer and tennis courts open all year.

Preston Park
A large park north of the station and beloved of locals who use the cycle track and eat at the two cafés. The park is a showpiece for municipal bedding, has a formal rose garden, a croquet lawn and a recently replanted Edwardian walled garden at Preston Manor (see page 43), which stands within the park. The children's playground incorporates a roller-blading area and there are tennis courts and a bowling green. Opposite the park is Preston Rock Garden, with rockeries laid out according to the famous 'Willow Pattern' china.

SHOPPING

Think of something, anything you might want. A Cartier watch or a simple gemstone necklace; a kitsch plastic toy or beautiful silk underwear; a sculpture for your hallway or a fake fur cushion – it is there, waiting for you, in Brighton. Just when you think you've seen it all, another shop opens in this most cosmopolitan of British cities. There's retro chic, retro punk and retro just about anything else you can think of. Sophisticated flowers bloom bravely next to studded neckbands, bowls of glistening olives line up not far away from bright pink, lettered rock.

Shi-Shi (page 58)

With all this choice your head could be whirling, so we've done some of the hard work for you. The main kinds of shops are listed and what you might expect to find where. We've picked out some of the individual shops but there are more – many more. Plunge bravely in – you'll love it.

Starting from the top of the town, the funkiest and zaniest shops are to be found in the network of small streets that radiate down from the station and Trafalgar Street, known collectively as North Laine (see page 42). The big high-street names are to be found on the west side of town in and around the Churchill Square Shopping Centre (map C4–C5). In East Street (map E5) are upmarket clothes and hoe shops such as Reiss, The Glasshouse, Jones, Coast, Phase Eight and Russell and Bromley. They're all just a step away from the shop-lined twisting tangle of pathways – The Lanes.

Antiques, art galleries and bric-a-brac
Bond Street; map D4
Artrepublic has a good stock of contemporary work and prints.

Gloucester Road; map D2
Brighton Architectural Salvage is where you'll find that garden statue, lead urn, period fireplace or imposing chimneypiece.

Kensington Gardens; map D3
Snoopers Paradise is probably the right name for this huge jumbly shop

Bigart (page 54)

full of everything you've heard of and a lot you haven't, from retro clothes, furniture and jewellery to knick-knacks and strange ornaments.

Meeting House Lane; map D4/5

Here is the Brighton Lanes Antiques Centre, which will keep you happily rummaging for an hour or so.

Prince Albert Street; map D5

Here you'll find the Chameleon Gallery, showing contemporary paintings, and the Window Gallery, which displays crafts as well as paintings.

Trafalgar Street; map D2

Moth sells the loveliest old furniture, while Bigart has arty photographs and contemporary work.

Union Street; map D4/5

Dermot and Jill Palmer Antiques has mostly French and Jill furniture and furnishings (from bubblegum machines to wing armchairs and marble busts) set out nicely on three floors.

Books and Music

Brighton Square; map D4
Essential Music and Rounder Records are conveniently close together in the heart of The Lanes.

Duke Street; map C4–C5

Colin Page sells antique and rare second-hand books, but also a good selection of paperbacks, displayed outside the shop. You might also find that record or CD you've been looking for at The Classical Longplayer in this street.

Brighton Books

Kensington Gardens; map D3

There's no doubting what Brighton Books sell – they have an excellent selection of second-hand titles as do Sandpiper Books and Oxfam Books, which sell records as well. Resident stocks CDs, vinyl and art – and tickets to current gigs and concerts too. The Vintage Magazine Co is where you'll pick up not only classic mags but also such oldie joys as images of Dorothy from *The Wizard of Oz* and Betty Boop.

PICTURE POSTS
Each 95p
Colour Covers
Each £1.50
Please Handle
With Great Care

Resident (page 54)

New Road; map D4
T-shirts for tiny boys with slogans such as 'I Must Not Kiss the Girls' are among the many tempting lines for the very small in Foley and Finch.

North Road; map D3
Daisy Daisy is a classy second-hand shop for kids with lots of sought-after labels on the rails.

Sydney Street; map E2
You can't miss Cat and Mouse with its bright pink shop front, full of cool clothes for small kids from designers such as Oilily, Timberland, Oshgosh and Cakewalk.

Sydney Street; map D2/E2
David's Books is another good shop with new and second-hand books on all topics for browsers and buyers.

Trafalgar Street; map D2
Trafalgar Bookshop is where you'll find anything from an old *Lion* annual to excellent collections of paperbacks, ranging from J.G. Ballard to William Burroughs.

Children's clothes
Brighton Square; map D4
The Fairy Kingdom is full of sparkly and pretty dresses for little girls – and other fairy mementos too.

Cat and Mouse

Choccywoccydoodah (page 58)

Chocolates
Duke Street; map C4–C5
You won't believe your eyes when you happen upon Choccywoccydoodah, tucked away down this little street. Elaborate chocolate creations, cakes and sculpted chocolate look too good to be true. 'Divine, bespoke and decadent', says the sign outside, and they're right. Just don't go inside if you're hungry – it might all be too much. 'Don't panic, it's organic' reads the sign outside Montezuma's Chocolate, where you can also buy moody-blue fudge and ice cream.

Gardner Street; map D3
Botanica has wonderful chocolates, including organic chocs, sugar-free chocs and vegan ones.

Meeting House Lane; map D4
Sweet Williams sells home-made fudge, toffee crumble and chocolate explosion, among other sweet treats.

Fashion
Bond Street; map D4
Fans of Hampstead Bazaar will find their favourite shop here. Not catering for quite the same market is hippy-chick heaven Greenwich Village, with stalls stocking shawls, bags, children's dresses, kimonos and saris. Much more English rose is Lavender Room with not only clothes and lingerie but also cushions, throws and spreads.

Brighton Square; map D4
You'll find lots to drool over at Bugatto, where they stock rather lovely Italian shoes and boots. And if you're going clubbing or partying, Aneela Rose is full of wonderful glittery and glam creations – handmade halter-neck tops, embroidered jeans and floaty dresses with an Eastern touch.

Dukes Lane; map C5
Profile, with several doorways opening into this narrow lane, has a comprehensive collection of classic clothes, shoes and accessories for men.

Duke Street; map D4
If you want an outfit that will stand out in the crowd, visit the shop called Old Village – you can't fail. And perhaps a look in Motto, with classy clothes and lovely shoes from L'Autre Chose, will put the icing on the cake.

East Street; map E5
'Style is not a question of age and size', says the heart-warming sign in The Glasshouse, which claims to stock clothes for 'real women'. I.S.C. Woman sells designer labels such as Nougat and French Connection.

Gardner Street; map D3
Going clubbing? Electric Rock has three floors of tempting gear.

Gloucester Road; map D2
You might like to worship at Shi-Shi Shoe Temple where beautiful footwear is lovingly displayed. Not far away is Covet selling pretty clothes and hats.

Shi-Shi

Electric Rock

Kensington Gardens; map D3

If you're under a certain age you'll be spoilt for choice in this busy lane, where many shops spill out onto the pavement. Young labels such as Zero, Pig and Flip can be found at Oddballs and there's a good choice at DOT DOT DOT and Get Cutie.

Good retro, alternative and second-hand gear is waiting at Rokit, while Yellow Submarine is full of sought-after '70s gear including Gola and Lonsdale. Todds of Brighton offers stylish designer labels including Duck and Cover, Escada Sport, Kenvelo and Mura (for men).

Why spend a lot of money on clothes that not many people see? You'll know why if you peer into the window of Nilaya which sells the most beautiful lingerie as well as lovely bags and scarves. Specs, with its eye-catching displays, is where you'll find Diesel, Gucci and D&G sunglasses.

Specs (page 59)

T-shirt shop

North Street; map D4

If you're not on a tight budget, you can't go wrong at Froggett, which stocks beautiful clothes for all occasions.

Meeting House Lane; map D5

Hat Heaven is where you buy hats, of course.

Pool Valley; map E5

Revisions is the place to go for nearly-new designer gear from Gucci to Galliano.

Sydney Street; map E5

Want to cut a dash with a '50s neckerchief or an old pair of 501s? Look in To Be Worn Again and the chances are you can. Solar is full of clubbing gear and hoodies. Minky Minky sells lovely slinky clothes, shoes, bags and cool sun specs,

while you can visit Poison for all your Rocky Horror requirements, including comb-in hair colour, studded collars and fishnets.

More clubbing and party gear at Magick with its bright bodices, Hedos handbags and extravagant costume jewellery.

Solar

Botanica

Planted

Flowers and plants

Gardner Street; map D3
Botanica is full of both beautiful flowers as well as chocolates (see page 58).

St James's Street; map F5
Planted has so many unusual and classy plants and flowers that they spill out onto the pavement, brightening up the street corner.

Sydney Street; map E2
Gunn's Flowers (established in 1876) is a

Brighton institution but keeps well ahead of the times with fresh displays at all of its outlets, which include this colourful shop and one in Castle Square (map E5).

Trafalgar Street; map D2
This street is home to Flower Design, who not only make up bouquets but also sell elegant pots and all the bits and pieces that create the right setting for displaying plants and flowers indoors.

Food
See Markets (page 68) and Delicatessens (page 72).

Gift shops
Bond Street; map D4
Tsena has a wide range of stylish gifts, including candles, handmade ceramics, glassware, and pretty clothes and shoes for babies.

Brighton Square; map D4
Marinposa is where you'll find a huge selection of nicely made Italian pottery.

Kensington Gardens; map D3
Appendage sells funky designer jewellery along with eye-catching bags, ceramics, stoneware and glassware. And, if you're into juggling, roller-blading or have a yen for yo-yos, visit Oddballs where they will see that you get what you want.

Meeting House Lane; map D5
Anyone would like a present from Pecksniffs, whose classy bath oils, candles, body lotions and scents look as good as they smell. Pure South sells African jewellery and bead work.

Juggling at Oddballs

Pavilion Buildings; map E4
The Royal Pavilion gift shop is one of the best in the business, with unusual books and objects but also many original figurines from Rye Pottery and some beautiful copies of china and glass from the collection inside the Pavilion. The nearby Museum has a well-stocked gift shop, too.

Sydney Street; map E2
Cissie Mo sells inventive plastic items, from ashtrays and boxes to pretty lights and woollies for pet pooches. Anyone who enjoys scribbling would love a Lamy pen, leather writing case or some handmade paper from Pen to Paper. The famous Brighton Bead Shop has glass ones, plastic ones, big

Pecksniffs

Velvet

ones, small ones — and you can make all sorts of things with them.

Brighton Bead Shop

Trafalgar Street; map E2
Here is the much-loved Workshop Pottery run by Peter Stocker, who makes the colourful earthenware and ceramic pots, mugs, plates, jugs and bowls on display.

House and Garden
Bond Street; map D4
Always wanted a garden gnome (they're rather chic now)? Try Bluebell, where you'll also find barbecues, ornamental metal jugs and pink flamingos. Ananda stocks furniture, rugs,

throws, cushions and folk art from Java. And if you're into velvet that's exactly what you'll find at Velvet, where you can buy a whole host of objects made from the material.

Castle Square; map E5
Hare Interiors sells cool and crisp bed and table linen and things for the home along with Farrow and Ball paints and wallpapers, while Cologne and Cotton concentrates on

linens, quilts, throws and things that smell good.

George Street; map F5
At Home with Miss Jones has a window full of objects perfect for town gardens — pots, snail and angel sculptures and tealight holders.

Gloucester Road; map D2
Yashar Bish is the right-sounding name for a shop selling lovely rugs, kelims and oriental pots.

Bluebell

Brighton Retro Furniture

textiles, lighting, mirrors and other goodies while England at Home is another place to look for something different. Steamer Trading sells all manner of kitchen goods, including great espresso-making machines.

Sydney Street; map E2

Brighton Retro Furniture is where you can buy back that Susie Cooper coffee set you got rid of 20 years ago, or invest in a set of folding leather chairs. There's plenty of choice of furniture from around the world at Villa and Hut.

Villa and Hut

Kensington Gardens; map D3

Cool and groovy, if you use that sort of language, is how you would describe Roost, which stocks everything for stylish living. Designer radios, clocks, mirrors, lamps and furniture are all here.

New Road; map D4

Lots of household goodies

in Mr Smith Interiors.

Prince Albert Street; map D5

Pad Furniture has solid old chests, colourful wall hangings, antique Indian mirrors and silk bedspreads with gold thread embroidery.

Ship Street; map D5

Vanilla sells unusual

Jewellery

Jewellery is what Brighton does better than any-where – especially in The Lanes. Listed here are a few of the many good jewellers in town.

Brighton Square; map D4

Gold Coast sells every-thing from collectable second-hand watches to stylish pieces in contem-porary settings.

Gloucester Road; map D2

Julian Stephens Gallery and Workshop has beauti-ful contemporary silver by individual jewellers; items include make-up brushes and boxes.

Kensington Gardens; map D2

Don't expect to find gold and silver in the aptly named Rock Pools, but a beautiful selection of

necklaces, bracelets and brooches made out of minerals, stones and shells. The soft pinks and purples of rose quartz and amethyst contrast with sea-washed green stones to give the most lovely colour combinations.

Meeting House Lane; map D4–D5

There are lots of unusual rings in the window of

Silverado

Rock Pools

Paul Goble (Jewellers and Pawnbrokers) while Grains of Gold and Turning Heads both have beautifully designed contemporary jewellery on display. Unusual and pretty gemstone necklaces are displayed in the window of Soma. If you want something really

Air Born Kites (page 68)

over the top and sparkly, go to All That Glitters, with its costume jewellery – including tiaras. The Lanes Jewellers has not only very unusual necklaces but also many collectable Moorcroft vases. Silverado sells – yes – silver, from around the world, while Avatar has some fine necklaces and bracelets.

St James's Street; map F5
Beautiful designs in silver, titanium and stainless steel are to be had at Spiral.

Union Street; map D5
This is where you'll find Michael Rose and Harry Diamond (who else?) and Son, selling a huge range of rings, brooches, earrings and necklaces.

Toys
Bond Street; map D4
You might think you're going crazy when you walk past The Animal House, but you're probably OK – the jungly noises ARE coming from the shop, which sells all sorts of toy animals, from cats, mice and butterflies to cuddly tigers and lions.

Potter's Children's Store

Yummies has lovely children's toys from scaled-down tools to tea sets.

Brighton Square; map D5
Here you'll find the Winnie-the-Pooh Shop, while broken dolls and teddy bears receive attention at Sue Pearson's Dolls and Teddy Bears, where you can buy new ones or take old ones for treatment at the 'hospital'.

Gardner Street; map D3
Children (not to mention

many adults too) will almost certainly like a colourful flying object from Air Born Kites.

Meeting House Lane; map D5
Potter's Children's Store

sells all those traditional toys and games that young people still love today.

Markets
Plenty of these in Brighton, including the huge Sunday Market in the Station car park (9.00–14.00). This popular market has stalls ranging from antiques, clothes and toys to food, plants and bits and pieces sold from car boots. The Saturday morning antique and craft stalls (sometimes open during the week) are a draw in Upper Gardner Street (map D3).

The Open Market, sells everything from fruit and veg, cheese and fish to baby clothes and equipment, haberdashery, Thai and Indian foods, and plants and flowers. It is held daily off the London Road. The Brighton Flea Market in Kemp Town is also held daily.

> **TREAT YOURSELF**
> Retro is what we once rejected but now feel a great nostalgia for. You can indulge those memories in the North Laine, where you'll find glass-fronted cocktail cabinets, formica-topped tables, Susie Cooper coffee sets and strange-shaped televisions.

EATING AND DRINKING

The Curve Bar (page 71)

Brighton is awash with places to eat and drink. Bars, café-bars, restaurants – you would be unlucky not to find what you fancied. It's obligatory to try the fish and chips on the pier, while the choice of Italian restaurants is so large it's hard to avoid a good pizza. They do vegetarian very well indeed, with award-winning restaurants and good-humoured bars and cafés serving delicious meatless meals. The list below is not comprehensive – but should help stave off the hunger pangs.

CAFES

Brighton Square; map D4
The cakes at Henny's Café, where you can eat in or outside by the fountain, are just the thing after a hard hour's shopping in The Lanes. They do good deli sandwiches too.

Brunswick Street East, Hove
The Sanctuary Café is just that, with vegetarian food and great coffee and cake.

Gardner Street; map D3
The Curve Bar, attached to the Komedia Theatre, serves coffee all day, and food. There's an Internet café upstairs.

Gloucester Road; map D2
Inside and Out is a tiny coffee shop and café with tasty breakfast foods and lunchtime salads, soups and fresh orange juice. You can sit on the raised terrace outside and watch while the world below goes shopping.

Inside and Out

Wai Kika Moo Kau

INTERNET CAFES

There is no shortage of Internet cafés in Brighton. These are just some of them: Internet Junction, 109 Western Road and 101 St George's Road (in Kemp Town); The Curve Bar, Gardner Street; Eazinet, West Street; Pursuit Internet, Preston Street; Riki Tiks, Bond Street; and Sumo, Middle Street.

Meeting House Lane; map D5

Wai Kika Moo Kau needs to be said very quickly before you get the joke. No dairy produce here but they do 'soyachinos' (coffee with soya milk). Try the couscous salad with toasted pine nuts and herbs. There's another branch in Kensington Gardens in the North Laine area (map D3).

The End of the Lane café is, as you would expect, at the end of the lane.

Old Steine; map E5

If your name was Frank, what else would you call a café here but Frank in Steine? They serve good coffee and sandwiches.

Trafalgar Street; map E2

Coffee – and more – at Crust and, nearby, Toast.

The Lanes Deli and Pasta Shop

DELICATESSENS

Try Bona Foodie (get it?) in St James's Street (map F5) for delicious hand-made pies (chicken, mushroom, tarragon and leek, or game), while in the same street the Cherry Tree Mediterranean Deli has wonderful Italian ice cream. Back in the centre of town, The Lanes Deli and Pasta Shop has a mouth-watering selection of food. In Trafalgar Street, in the North Laine, you'll find the Real Patisserie, while the North Laine Deli is close by in Kensington Gardens.

RESTAURANTS
Asian, Japanese and Chinese
China China
**74 Preston Street;
map A4/5**
Good authentic Chinese food at low prices.
Tel: 01273 328028

China Garden
**88 Preston Street;
map A4**

Pricey but worth it. The food is delicious and you eat to discreet live music from the resident pianist.
Tel: 01273 325124

E-Kagen Sushi and Noodle Café
**23 Sydney Street;
map E2**
Café above the Yum-Yum Oriental Market serving good fast noodles at very reasonable prices.
Tel: 01273 606777

Gar's
**19 Prince Albert Street;
map D5**
This restaurant is popular with theatre-goers, both before and after the show. Nothing out of the ordinary on this Chinese menu, but a lively atmosphere and pleasant service.
Tel: 01273 321321

Krakatoa
**7 Pool Valley, The Lanes;
map E5**
You can sit at Japanese-style tables upstairs although the food is a mix of Thai, Indonesian and Japanese. Choices include sushi and deep fried squid in crispy batter served with chilli sambal.
Tel: 01273 719009

Moshi Moshi

Moshi Moshi
Bartholomew Square, The Lanes; map D5
Ultra-modern sushi restaurant opposite the Visitor Information Centre. You can sample sushi and all sorts of hot delicacies — this is fast, healthy food, fresh from the conveyor belt.
Tel: 01273 719195

Fish
English's
29 East Street; map E5
Converted from fishermen's cottages, this is the restaurant once loved by Lawrence Olivier and Charlie Chaplin. Eat dinner inside or sit out in the square, listening to the jazz band.
Tel: 01273 327980

Harry Ramsden's
1–4 Marine Parade; map F5
Britain's best known fish and chippy with a lot more to offer, including Yorkshire pudding and

TREAT YOURSELF
Visit the Hotel du Vin in Ship Street, Havana in Duke Street or, if you're into sushi, the colourful Moshi Moshi in Bartholomew Square for a special meal. Vegetarians and carnivores alike may treat themselves at Terre à Terre in East Street or the Brighton favourite, Food For Friends, in Prince Albert Street.

onion gravy. But you go here for haddock and chips (cooked in beef dripping) and cups of Yorkshire tea.
Tel: 01273 690691

Loch Fyne Oyster Bar and Restaurant
95 Western Road; map B4
Part of the growing chain of fish restaurants taking the Scottish loch as their theme. Good reliable cooking (such as haddock chowder and sea bass with lime and coriander).
Tel: 01273 716160

The Regency
King's Road, Brighton seafront; map A5
Fresh fish simply cooked is what the Regency, overlooking the sea and the picturesque West Pier, has always done best. From grilled sardines, scallops

and lemon sole to excellent fish and chips – you can't go wrong. And, if you're interested, the building used to be the home of Harriet Mellon, once the richest woman in Europe and widow of banker Thomas Coutts.
Tel: 01273 325014

French
Hotel du Vin
Ship Street; map D5
This, the fifth hotel and bistro in the award-winning mini-chain, thrives on the same formula as those in Winchester, Bristol, Birmingham, Harrogate and Tunbridge Wells. The food is French with an emphasis on quality – the menu changes daily to reflect what's good in the market, and the wines are terrific.
Tel: 01273 718588

Italian
Al Duomo
7 Pavilion Buildings; map E4
One of Brighton's favourites, with reliable pizzas (from the wood-fired oven), pastas and other Italian dishes. Cheerful, welcoming and child-friendly.
Tel: 01273 760617

Al Forno
36 East Street, The Lanes; map E5
Another traditional Italian restaurant where they welcome children, don't present you with an enormous bill and give you friendly service.
Tel: 01273 324905

Bella Napoli
2 Village Square, Brighton Marina
Family-run pasta and pizza house with excellent wines, lovely ice cream and aromatic coffee.
Tel: 01273 818577

Donatello
1 Brighton Place, The Lanes; map D5
The biggest in a family of pizzerias in Brighton but coping perfectly with the impressive number of meals they produce on a

Donatello

daily basis. Efficient and friendly service with a special small-portion menu for children.
Tel: 01273 775477

La Veramente
28 Church Road,
Hove
Mediterranean food with specials that include grilled whole sea bass and lamb with honey, garlic and rosemary sauce.
Tel: 01273 720008

Leonardo
55 Church Road,
Hove
Classy cooking – try the risottos – and excellent service and value.
Tel: 01273 328888

Pinocchio's
22 New Road; map D4
Popular with the pre-theatre crowd, this is another well-run restaurant that is part of the Donatello chain and just as lively and welcoming as the others.
Tel: 01273 677676

Sole Mio
64 Western Road,
Hove
Upmarket Italian with a Spanish influence. Once a branch of the NatWest

bank, the restaurant is light and airy and the food is a bit special.
Tel: 01273 770093

Topolino Duo
67 Church Road,
Hove
Bright, friendly and pleasant Italian restaurant, café/bar.
Tel: 01273 749490

Mexican
Santa Fe
East Street; map E5
Stylish surroundings and delicious shrimp tacos, shrimp ceviche or a lime and green chilli salmon make for a good evening out.
Tel: 01273 823231

Brighton Rocks

Modern European
Brighton Rocks
6 Rock Place, Kemp Town
Wonderful colourful salads, fresh fish and meat

with a Mediterranean influence. Nice seaside feel on the sunny terrace and inside the stylish bar/restaurant is popular with gay couples.
Tel: 01273 601139

Browns
3 Duke Street; map C4
Browns is Browns in Oxford, Edinburgh, Bristol, Cambridge and so forth, but it's always good fun and reliable. Excellent coffee and service.

Ha! Ha! Bar and Canteen
2 Pavilion Buildings;
map E4
In a prime position next to the Pavilion Gardens, this is the place to sit with a coffee, linger over a plate of pasta, dive into a carrot and smoky aubergine dip, or down a beer or two.
Tel: 01273 737080

Havana
32 Duke Street,
The Lanes; map C4
They take the colonial theme seriously here with wicker and cream chairs, but there's no doubt about the quality of the food. Try monkfish with rosti and fennel, or pappardelle of wild mushrooms topped with shaved (what

Havana

else?) Parmesan. You can sit inside the restaurant or outside.
Tel: 01273 773388

No Name Restaurant Bar
82 St James's Street; map F5
This one has no name, so it gets called – you've got it. Dishes like fresh black figs with buffalo mozzarella or scallops on the shell with tomato, coriander and ginger salsa make it worth remembering the no-name bit.
Tel: 01273 693216

Quod
160 North Street; map D4
Fresh from its triumphs in Oxford and London, Quod brings its chargrills, fish, pastas and risottos – and its spectacular paintings on the walls – to

Brighton. Cannellini beans with rocket and cherry tomatoes, confit of duck with celeriac, or roasted monkfish wrapped in cured ham are other dishes to enjoy.
Tel: 01273 202070

Seven Dials
1–3 Buckingham Place; map B1
Effortlessly good cooking with flair and imagination. Try goats' cheese on lentil cake, or carrot soup with roasted pumpkin seeds. Just the place for dinner on a special occasion.
Tel: 01273 885555

Thai
Aumthong Thai
60 Western Road, Hove
Beautifully costumed staff to match the very good

food. It's always busy, so best to book.
Tel: 01273 773922

Sawadee
87 St James's Street; map F5
Try mussels steamed in lemongrass, sweet basil and chilli, or sea bass with lime and coriander dressing. Modern surroundings and good food.
Tel: 01273 624233

Sing Tong Thai at the Pond
49 Gloucester Road; map D2
The Pond is a busy (and bright blue) pub – the Thai restaurant is a small room upstairs serving good red and green curries and noodles. They do takeaway too.
Tel: 01273 621400

Sing Song Thai

Food For Friends

Foodwrks

Foodwrks
48 Queen's Road; map C3
How about lemon tart with gin glaze? Or aubergine parcels with grilled tomato relish? That's the sort of food you'll find here – plus the most delicious cakes.
Tel: 01273 724873

The George
Trafalgar Street; map E2
Smart but unpretentious little pub on the sunny side of the street serving delicious dishes such as tomato, tarragon and orange cassoulet; aubergine cannelloni; and veggie bangers and mash served up with rich onion gravy, and chickpea and potato cakes.
Tel: 01273 681055

Vegetarian
Food For Friends
17 Prince Albert Street; map D5
The 'Friends' bit comes when you share plates of mini samosas with an onion salad, Japanese tempura with ginger dipping sauce, olives, and feta with deep fried lavash bread. The food is innovative, delicious and very popular while the restaurant, with its huge windows, provides as much interest for those looking out as those looking in.
Tel: 01273 202310

The George (page 77)

Terre à Terre
East Street; map E5

This highly acclaimed restaurant draws people from all over who forget they are meat-eaters. There's an imaginative choice, from smoked sakini soba salad, buttered squeak and Shropshire (cheese) sausage to truffled potato and celeriac puree. Do you know what an ash crotin and parsley shooter is? Come here and find out.
Tel: 01273 729051

PUBS
The Basketmaker's Arms
Gloucester Road; map E2

What this well-kept pub lacks in space it makes up for in atmosphere. The food is good and unpretentious – hot salt beef on granary, home-cooked fish and chips on Fridays, bangers (meat or veggie) and mash with onion gravy, and very good sandwiches. It serves Gales Bitter, HSB, guest beers and a huge selection of malt whiskies.

The Basketmaker's Arms

Bath Arms
Union Street/Meeting House Lane; map D5

Claiming to be the oldest licensed premises in town, this many-roomed pub is nicely furnished and decorated with old photographs and prints. Straightforward bar food, good wine and a selection of real ales.

Colonnade
New Road; map D4

You can't miss the pub's connections with the Theatre Royal next door. It's red-plush Victorian, cosy, comfortable and well run.

The Cricketers
Black Lion Street; map D5

Three hundred years or so ago this was called 'The Laste and Fishcart' because of its proximity to a fish market (a laste is a measure of fish). It was

The Cricketers

DR BRIGHTON'S
This seafront pub was once a hotel, built in the late 18th century. It takes its name from William Thackeray's description of the town as 'kind, cheerful, merry Dr Brighton'.

then bought by a Mr Jutten, a cricketer, who changed the name. Now it's a well-run town pub with a nice Victorian feel. There's bar food and a separate restaurant.

Dr Brighton's
King's Road; map D5
Gay pub that is not cliquey. If you fancy flavoured schnapps, you'll be in heaven.

The Hand in Hand
St James's Street; map F5

Meeting Place Café

There's not a lot of room here, so you'll need to take a deep breath and slip in sideways, but then you can soak up some atmosphere and their own-brewed beer.

Mash Tun
Church Street; map D4
Pub with sofas upstairs, chairs down below; you can read newspapers, drink coffee and eat, too.

Mrs Fitzherbert's
New Road; map D4
Cosy town pub in a busy street. Good for pre- or post-theatre drinks or snacks.

Three Jolly Butchers
North Road, North Laine; map D3
This is a pub, although you're not sure until you look inside. The food's excellent too.

> ### TREAT YOURSELF
> **Stroll along the seafront towards Hove. When you see the Meeting Place Café stop and have a coffee and one of their famous toasted sandwiches. This is where Brighton ends and Hove begins – or the other way around. The wonderful Regency buildings on the landward side make up the famous Brunswick Square and the tall angel is the Peace Statue.**

NIGHTLIFE

If clubbing's your thing, you've come to one of the best places in the UK. But don't stay in if it's not. Brighton has plenty of theatres, good cinemas and comedy clubs and probably the biggest selection of bars and restaurants in any UK city. So – dress up, dress down – enjoy yourself.

On the town

You'll know where to go if you're into clubbing. Here are a few of the best known – but you'll find plenty more. The Beach at King's Road Arches (map D6; tel: 01273 722272) right on the seafront is a favourite beach bar by day, and throbs at night as Brighton's clubbers queue to get in. Not far away in the Arches are the Funky Buddha Lounge (tel: 01273 725541), which is smaller and stylish, and the sophisticated Honey Club (tel: 01273 446939). If you feel nostalgic you should visit Zap – Brighton's oldest club – also in King's Road Arches and still going strong (tel: 01273 202407). The Escape, away from the seafront in Marine Parade, (map F5; tel: 01273 606906) is Brighton's favourite. Modern jazz is the thing at The Jazz Rooms in Ship Street (map D5; tel: 01273 321692).

A night at the theatre

When the Prince Regent ordered the construction of a huge domed space to house his beloved horses, he can hardly have guessed it would become one of Brighton's top performance venues. The Dome in Church Street (map E4) in fact comprises three halls – the Concert Hall, the Corn Exchange and the Pavilion Theatre. The shows range from music of all sorts to dance,

> ### TREAT YOURSELF
> Every night, about an hour before the sun sets, there's a spectacular display of flying over the sea between Brighton Pier and West Pier as millions of starlings return to the latter to roost for the night. Buy yourself a long drink, settle down in a deckchair and enjoy the aerobatics.

opera, theatre – you name it. Tel: 01273 709709 or visit the website www.brighton-dome.org.uk.

Gardner Arts, Sussex University's theatre in Lewes Road, Falmer (tel: 01273 685861), is strong on new material, film and produces excellent children's shows. Komedia in Gardner Street (map D3; tel: 01273 647100 or visit www.komedia.co.uk.) in the heart of North Laine is a popular venue for fringe theatre and has excellent comedy and regular shows for kids. It is well served by its café, The Curve. The New Venture Theatre at Bedford Place (tel: 01273 746118 or visit www.newventure.org.uk) is a showcase for new writing and innovative directing. Brighton's oldest theatre is the Theatre Royal in New Road (map D4; tel: 01273 328488 or visit the website www.theambassadors.com/brighton). It has a varied range of drama and music.

Komedia

Go to a movie
The Duke of York's Picture House in Preston Circus (tel: 01273 602503 or 626261 for recorded information) is a Brighton favourite. An independent cinema, it shows many one-night-only films and many you have longed to see again. Brighton Cinemateque in Middle Street (map C5; tel: 01273 384300) in The Lanes is not open every night, so ring in advance for details. They show films no one else does, from silent movies to Russian drama. The Odeon in West Street (map C5; tel: 0870 5050007) has several screens and an excellent ice-cream café. The UGC Marina at the Marina (tel: 08701 555145) is the latest multiplex and shows all the new films.

TOURS AND TRIPS

Brighton is not a large city and the best way to enjoy it is on foot. But you'll see a lot by spending a few pounds on a 'hop on – hop off' open-top bus tour. You'll gain a different perspective entirely from a boat trip or you can hire a cycle and enjoy a hassle-free pedal along the Hove cycle lane.

Ghost Walk

MODS AND ROCKERS

Brighton beach was the battle-ground for the infamous clash between the 'mods' on their scooters and the 'rockers' on their motor-bikes in 1964. The whole culture of mods and rockers was captured in the cult film *Quadrophenia*, much of which was made in Brighton.

On foot

A whole series of guided walks are on offer through Blue Badge guides. For details, call into the Visitor Information Centre (VIC) in Bartholomew Square, or telephone them on 0906 7112255. Glenda Clarke is a Blue Badge guide who offers a year-round Ghost Walk on the first Saturday of every month and at Halloween. She will also guide pre-booked groups on a summer Quadrophenia Walk with behind-the-scenes information on The Who's cult classic film about the mods and rockers mayhem more than 40 years ago. Pre-booked groups can enjoy the secrets of The Lanes with her, or go on a Murder Walk or a Rich and Famous Tour. For details, telephone her on 01273 888596 or visit www.brightonwalks.com.

By bus

You'll see the bright red 'city sightseeing' buses throughout Brighton. You can buy a ticket from the driver or from the Visitor Information Centre in Bartholomew Square. The tickets are valid for 24 hours and include a taped commentary. The eleven stops include Brighton Pier, the Marina and the Royal Pavilion. Details on 01789 294466 or visit the website www.city-sightseeing.com.

On the water

At Brighton Marina you'll find licensed charter boats with professional skippers, who will take individuals and parties out fishing during the day and for evening sightseeing trips. You're welcome to take a picnic and there are facilities for disabled visitors. Telephone Mike Snelling for bookings or further information on 01273 307700 or 07973 38679 or visit www.girlgray.com. You can arrange coastal cruises, sea trips, harbour tours and fishing trips through Dave Wilson of Marina Water Tours. Telephone 07958 246414 or 01273 818237, or visit www.watertours.co.uk.

Brighton Races

Brighton Racecourse is one of the oldest in the country – racing's been going on here on Whitehawk Down with its wonderful views over Brighton and Hove for well over 200 years. There are more than 20 fixtures between April and October with special events and attractions for the whole family. Telephone 01273 603580 for information.

Go to the dogs

There are several evening meetings each week at the Greyhound Stadium in Nevill Road, Hove. It has a licensed restaurant, bars and a snack bar, and children are welcome. Telephone 01273 204601 for details.

WHAT'S ON

Almost the whole of May is given over to the annual Brighton Festival, which in turn has spawned a 'fringe' just as lively and exciting. But Brighton never closes for business and, whatever time of the year you visit, you'll find something going on.

For more information on events, call in at the Visitor Information Centre (see page 94) or visit: www.visitbrighton.com, www.brighton.co.uk or www.theinsight.co.uk

January
Holiday on Ice
Brighton Centre;
Tel: 01273 290131

February
Sussex Beacon half-marathon
Starts and finishes in Madeira Drive;
Tel: 0906 7112255

March
Pioneer Motorcycle Ride
From Epsom Downs to Madeira Drive;
Tel: 0906 7112255

April
Morris Minor Rally
Madeira Drive;
Jaguar Promenade
Madeira Drive;
Tel: 0906 7112255

May
Brighton Festival
Hundreds of events, including a children's parade, dance, performance art, theatre, recitals, concerts, exhibitions and opera, at various venues. Don't miss the Horse-driving Trials at Stanmer Park, or the Mackerel Fayre and Blessing of the Nets on the seafront.
Tel: 0906 7112255

Sustainable Building Event and **Arts and Crafts for Children**
Weald and Downland Open Air Museum, Chichester;
Tel: 01243 811348
Website: www. wealddown.co.uk

June
Classic Car Show
Madeira Drive;
London to Brighton Bike Ride
Finishes in Madeira Drive;
Food and Drink Lovers' Festival (various venues);
Party in the Park

Sustainable Building Event

Preston Park;
Tel: 0906 7112255
Heavy Horse Spectacular
and **The Wood Show**
Weald and Downland
Open Air Museum,
Chichester;
Tel: 01243 811348
Website: www.
wealddown.co.uk

July
Kite Festival
Stanmer Park;
Tel: 0906 7112255
**Early Music Afternoon,
Open Air Theatre** and
**Rare and Traditional
Breeds Show**
Weald and Downland
Open Air Museum,
Chichester;
Tel: 01243 811348
Website: www.
wealddown.co.uk
Garden Weekend
Parham Gardens,
Pulborough;
Tel: 01903 744888
Website: www.
parhaminsussex.co.uk

August
Pride
Gay festival in Preston
Park;
Tel: 0906 7112255
Evening opening
at Parham Gardens,
Pulborough;
Tel: 01903 744888

Website: www.
parhaminsussex.co.uk
Rural history
Re-enactment at Weald
and Downland Open Air
Museum, Chichester;
Tel: 01243 811348
Website: www.
wealddown.co.uk

September
National Speed Trials
Madeira Drive;
Heritage Open Weekend
Brunswick Square and
other venues;
**Brighton Early Music
Festival** (various venues);
Tel: 0906 7112255
Autumn Flowers
at Parham House,
Pulborough
Tel: 01903 744888
Website: www.
parhaminsussex.co.uk

October
**Brighton Early Music
Festival** (various venues);
Jewish Film Festival
The Duke of York's Picture
House, Preston Circus and
Cinemateque, The Lanes;
One Live in Brighton
Radio One event;
Tel: 0906 7112255

**Autumn Countryside
celebration**
Weald and Downland
Open Air Museum,
Chichester;
Tel: 01243 811348
Website: www.
wealddown.co.uk

November
RAC Veteran Car Run
London to Brighton;
Cine City film festival;
Tel: 0906 7112255

December
Burning the Clocks
Winter solstice
celebration;
Tel: 0906 7112255
**Tree Dressing and Tastes
of a Tudor Christmas**
Weald and Downland
Open Air Museum,
Chichester;
Tel: 01243 811348
Website: www.
wealddown.co.uk

BRIGHTON FOR KIDS

Eleven kilometres (7 miles) of beach and probably the best pier in Britain, full of fun things to do, should be enough for most kids. But if these excitements pall, Brighton and Hove still have a lot in reserve.

'Gallopers' on the seafront

Life's a beach
At least it is in Brighton and although it's a pebbled one, the thrill of being by the sea keeps youngsters happy for hours on end.

The end of the pier show
Brighton Pier (see page 39) is brash, loud and full of naughty seaside gaiety – just what children want. There's candyfloss and rock, souvenirs, novelty kiosks, fish and chips and trays of seafood and – right at the end – a pretty good selection of fairground rides. Free deckchairs for mum and dad.

Octopus challenge
Are you are as clever as an octopus? You can find out at the Brighton Sea Life Centre (see page 39) in Marine Parade just across the road from Brighton Pier. The Centre has the longest underwater tunnel anywhere so that you can watch sharks, rays, giant turtles and

Paint Pots (page 87)

Fairground ride on Brighton Pier

other denizens of the deep. Learn to love crabs and sea anemones at the hourly 'hands-on' display at the rock pool and enjoy the antics of the sea turtles in their new home. And those clever octopuses? From the Giant Pacific octopus to the cuttlefish and nautilus, they're being taught how to open jars and find their way through a maze – and you'll see what quick learners they are.

A ride along the seafront

The charmingly old-fashioned Volks Electric Railway, which opened in 1883 and is still going strong, will take you along the seafront for 2 kilo-metres (1.2 miles) and drop you near the Marina.

Visit the wizard

You'll find him asleep in his hammock in his attic at Hove Museum and Art Gallery (see page 41). This interactive toy gallery, with trains rushing under the floor (you can see them through the 'windows') is great fun for every family member. Oh – and that funny noise you hear from time to time? It's the wizard, snoring.

Eating out

There are so many good restaurants and cafés in Brighton and Hove that finding child-friendly places is not a problem. Especially good are the Italian restaurants, like Donatello, Pinocchio's or Al Forno and Harry Ramsden's (see pages 73–75).

Paint your own

Paint Pots at 39 Trafalgar Street (map D2) is stacked full of plain plates, cups, mugs and bowls just waiting for children (or adults) to give them an individual touch. Paint on your own design and they'll fire it ready for you to pick up later. Ring them on 01273 833643.

Picnic in the park

Hove Park has a very good children's playground, a miniature railway that operates on some weekends, and lots of space for picnics.

OUT OF TOWN

If you can bear to tear yourself away from Brighton, there are plenty of interesting houses, gardens, museums – and the whole of the lovely South Downs – to explore just a very short distance away. Here are some suggestions to get you going.

Lewes

Lewes
10 miles east of Brighton, on the A27
This historic settlement, with its massive ruined Norman castle, is the county town of East Sussex. There's plenty to see, including Anne of Cleves house (given to her by Henry as part of her divorce settlement),

the Living History Model, telling the story of Lewes, and Lewes Priory ruins. As in Brighton, you'll find narrow walkways called 'twittens' and lots of antique shops.
Tel: (Tourist Information Centre) 01273 843 448
Website: www.lewes. gov.uk

Monks House
12 miles east of Brighton at Rodmell, off the A27 at Lewes
This is the tiny house where Virginia and Leonard Woolf lived, worked and entertained their literary friends. Now, it's owned by the National Trust and has a tenant, so it is open to the public

only at certain times.
Tel: 01892 890651
Website: www. nationaltrust.org.uk

Charleston, Firle
12 miles east of Brighton near Lewes, off the A27
This was where Bloomsbury artists Vanessa Bell and Duncan Grant moved with their extraordinary retinue of artistic and intellectual friends, family and lovers in the summer of 1916. They painted walls, doors, household objects and furniture, wove a tangled web of relationships and redesigned the garden. For more than half a century Charleston was at the heart of the Bloomsbury

Charleston

number 79 bus will take you there and back. If you want to walk the 11 kilometres (7 miles) to the Devil's Dyke, you can catch a number 77 back to the city. In Ditchling itself, 2.5 kilometres (1.5 miles) from the Beacon, there are loos, tea shops and pubs. Tel: 01273 292140 for information on 'bus walks'

Group's artistic and personal lives. You can see the house and garden and enjoy a themed guided tour on certain days of the week.
Tel: 01323 811626
Website:
www.charleston.org.uk

Bluebell Railway
16 miles north-east of Brighton at Sheffield Park, on the A275 Lewes to East Grinstead Road
Steam trains run between Sheffield Park Station, where there are locomotive sheds, a museum, gift shop and restaurant, and Kingscote. Pullman dining trains run most weekends. The service operates throughout the year but is limited during the winter.
Tel: 01825 720800 (general enquiries), 01825 722370 (talking timetable)

Website: www.bluebell-railway.co.uk

Ditchling Beacon
5 miles north of Brighton on the South Downs Way
Parking is not easy on this, the second highest point on the South Downs, but there are regular buses there and back from the city centre, so that you can enjoy a walk from the Beacon, which was an Iron Age hill fort. The

Borde Hill Garden
12 miles north of Brighton near Haywards Heath, via the A273 and B2036
This is not only a great 'plant-hunters' garden with an astonishing collection of trees, shrubs and fine specimens collected from around the world, but also home to a lovely rose garden and fine herbaceous planting. There are formal and informal areas,

Borde Hill Garden

a restored Victorian glasshouse, lakeside walk and a children's playground, plus shop and restaurant.
Tel: 01444 412151
Website: www.bordehill.co.uk

Wakehurst Place
20 miles north of Brighton at Ardingly, on the B2028 from Haywards Heath; entrance about one mile north of Ardingly

This is Kew in the country with 73 hectares (180 acres) of wonderful gardens and superb trees. It is also home to the new Millennium Seed Bank, which aims to save thousands of endangered plant species – an exhibition explains the project. Wakehurst is built round an Elizabethan manor, part of which is open, containing exhibition rooms, a gift shop and restaurant.
Tel: 01444 894066
Website: www.kew.org.uk

Tangmere Military Aviation Museum
20 miles west of Brighton, off the A27 near Chichester

This famous Battle of Britain airfield is now a museum telling the story of military flying from its earliest days up to the present time. There's special emphasis on the air war over southern England between 1939 and 1945. You can see all sorts of aircraft, including the Gloster Meteor in which Group Captain Teddy Donaldson set a new world air speed record of 986 kph (616 mph) in 1946 and the prototype Hawker Hunter, flown by Squadron Leader Neville Duke, which brought the record up to 1,163 kph (727 mph) in 1953.
Tel: 01243 775223
Website: www.tangmere-museum.org.uk

Weald and Downland Open Air Museum
30 miles west of Brighton at Singleton, off the A286 between Chichester and Midhurst

Here you'll find traditional rural buildings spanning six centuries, saved from destruction and moved to this lovely spot. There are hens and Shire horses and old breeds of sheep here, and display gardens show the herbs and plants our ancestors used for cooking, medicine and household purposes.
Tel: 01243 811348
Website: www.wealddown.co.uk

Weald and Downland Open Air Museum

WHERE TO STAY

Whatever the time of year people flock to Brighton, so it's hardly surprising to find a huge range of accommodation here. The Visitor Information Centre (see page 94) has a complete list of hotels, guest houses, bed and breakfasts, pubs, self-catering accommodation and caravan and camp sites. The list below will give you some idea of the range on offer. Check facilities and prices before booking.

Prices

The £ symbols are an approximate guide for comparing the prices charged for bed and breakfast, which range from about £25 to more than £100 per person per night.

The De Vere Grand
King's Road; map B5

Occupying a prime seafront position, this is Brighton's only five-star hotel, with 200 rooms and suites, indoor swimming pool, spa pool, gym, sauna, night club and restaurant. Tel: 01273 224300

Website: www. grandbrighton.co.uk
££££

Hotel du Vin
Ship Street; map D5

One hotel in the small, privately owned chain that leapt to acclaim in Winchester and has extended to other cities, including Tunbridge Wells and Harrogate. The hotels go for deep comfort without fuss. There are 34 bedrooms, and three suites with Egyptian linen sheets and monsoon-like showers. Good bar and

Hotel du Vin

The De Vere Grand

interesting food in the bistro (see page 74).
Tel: 01273 718588
Website: www.hotelduvin.com
£££

Nineteen
Broad Street; map F5
Stylish award-winner with just eight luxury bedrooms (ever slept in a glass bed before?). The emphasis is on comfort and pampering.
Tel: 01273 675529
Website: www.hotelnineteen.co.uk
£££

Topps Hotel
Regency Square; map A5
A small hotel in an attractive square. The 15 bedrooms all have en-suite facilities and there are two rooms with four-poster beds and balcony sea views.
Tel: 01273 729334
££/£££

Brightonwave
10 Madeira Place; map F5
Delicious buffet breakfasts at this stylishly furnished small guesthouse (six comfortable bedrooms) close to the sea.
Tel: 01273 676794
££/£££

New Steine Hotel
New Steine, Kemp Town
A warm, comfortable and brightly furnished hotel with 11 bedrooms. You can eat here too, at the bistro restaurant.
Tel: 01273 681546
Website: www.newsteinehotel.com
££

Churchill Guest House
Russell Square; map B4
Nine bedrooms at this friendly guesthouse in an attractive square, over-looking gardens but just a couple of minutes from the sea. The bedrooms all have en-suite facilities and you can choose from full English, continental or vegetarian breakfast.
Tel: 01273 700887
££

Elm Grove Farm
Streat Lane, Streat, near Plumpton, Hassocks
An extremely comfortable three-bedroomed bed and breakfast in this away-from-it-all listed Tudor farmhouse down a quiet country lane. Surrounded by meadows and a wonderful garden, this is a place for those seeking peace and quiet (no young children, dogs or smoking allowed) but only a short drive or train-ride from the city.
Tel: 01273 890368
££

University of Brighton
self-catering flats
Various locations
The Uni owns 50 well-equipped flats around the city, which are available from July to September. Good parking. Prices range from £86–£140 per week including electricity and linen. Contact them for a brochure.
Tel 01273 643167
Website: www.brighton.ac.uk

Elm Grove Farm

USEFUL INFORMATION

TOURIST INFORMATION

Visitor Information Centre (VIC), 10 Bartholomew Square, Brighton BN1 1JS, (map D5)
Services include accommodation booking, travel, attractions and events information, maps and guides.
Open: Mon–Fri 9.00–17.00, Sat 10.00–17.00, Sun 10.00–16.00 (no Sun opening Nov–Mar)
Tel: 0906 7112255 (calls cost 50p per minute standard rate)
Website: www. visitbrighton.com

What's on

The Argus is the local daily and carries listings, while The Source is a monthly listings publication that can be found in bars, cafés and shops. Visit the Visitor Information Centre (see above) or log on to www.brighton.co.uk.

Guided walks

For most Blue Badge guided walks, contact the Visitor Information Centre.
Ghost Walk: all year, 20.00 on first Sat of each month and Halloween;
Tel: 01273 888596

TRAVEL
Airport

The nearest airport is Gatwick.
Tel: 0870 000 2468

Bus and coach

The bus station is in Pool Valley (map E5).

National Express run direct services between London Victoria and Brighton (around two hours journey time).
Tel: 08705 808080

The local buses are modern, clean and comfortable. There's good timetable information at bus stops. You can either pay £1 for a flat-rate fare, or £2.50 for a day ticket that allows you to board any local service bus within the area bounded by Shoreham, Falmer and Newhaven.
Tel: 01273 886200
Website: www.buses.co.uk

Shopmobility

Churchill Square Shopping Centre (map C4–C5).
Brighton and Hove Shopmobility provides manual and powered wheelchairs and scooters.
Go to Churchill Car Park 1 Level. The charge is £3 per day.
Tel: 01273 323239

Taxis

The smartly liveried, aqua-blue-and-white taxis work 24 hours a day and can be hailed on the streets.
There are also taxi ranks in East Street (map D5), Queen Square (map C4; near the Clock Tower), in St James's Street (map F5) and outside Hove Town Hall in Church Road.

Trains

The railway station is in the city at Terminus Road, at the top of Queen's Road (map C1/D1). South

Central run regular services to Brighton from London Victoria (the fastest service is just 49 minutes). There are also regular trains (Thameslink) from London Kings Cross and London Bridge. Together they provide frequent trains to Haywards Heath, Gatwick and Luton airports.

National Rail Enquiry Service: 08457 484950

PARK AND RIDE
map: page 100
The Park and Ride is off the A23 at Withdean Stadium (sign-posted from the A23 and A27). Buses to and from the centre of Brighton leave every 12–15 minutes, Mon–Fri 7.36–6.12 and Sat 9.00–17.50. The fare is £2.40 with up to two children free. Parking is free.

Frequent trains run from Burgess Hill, Hassocks and Preston Park into the city. These stations all have car parks where you can leave your car.

BANKS
Cash dispensers:
Abbey National, St James's Street; map F5

Barclays, Church Road, Hove
HSBC, London Road;
HSBC, North Street;
map C5
Lloyds TSB, West Street;
map C4
Lloyds TSB Church Road, Hove
Royal Bank of Scotland, Castle Street; map A4
Woolwich, North Street; map C5

POST OFFICES
Brighton:
Ship Street; map D5
Trafalgar Street; map D2
St James's Street; map F5
Hove:
Blatchington Road

SPORT
King Alfred Leisure Centre, Kingsway, Hove
Tel: 01273 290290

Prince Regent Swimming Complex, Church Street; map E4
Tel: 01273 685692

Pulse Station, King's Road Arches (near West Pier) hire roller blades; map A5

Sussex Ice Rink, Queen Square, map C4
Tel: 01273 324677

EMERGENCIES
Fire, ambulance or police
Tel: 999

Brighton Police Station
John Street; map F4
Tel: 0845 6070999

Hove Police Station
Holland Road
Tel: 0845 6070999

Royal Sussex Hospital
Eastern Road (continuation of Edward Street), Kemp Town, (includes 24-hour accident and emergency department)
Tel: 01273 696955

NHS Direct
Tel: 0845 4647

Late-night pharmacies
These pharmacies stay open until 22.00:
Ashtons, Dyke Road, Seven Dials; map B1
Tel: 01273 325020
Westons, Coombe Terrace
Tel: 01273 605354

24-hour petrol station
Shell, Preston Road

24-hour emergency breakdown
Lee Hire, Church Place, Kemp Town
Tel: 01273 680044

INDEX

CITY-BREAK GUIDES

These full-colour guides come with stunning new photo-graphy capturing the essence of some of Britain's loveliest cities and towns. Each is divided into easy-reference sections where you will find something for everyone – from walk maps to fabulous shopping, from sightseeing highlights to keeping the kids entertained, from recommended restaurants to tours and trips ... and much, much more.

BATH

Stylish and sophisticated – just two adjectives that sum up the delightful Roman city of Bath, which saw a resurgence of popularity in Georgian times and in the 21st century is once again a vibrant and exciting place to be.

CAMBRIDGE

Historic architecture mingles with hi-tech revolution in the university city of Cambridge, where stunning skylines over surrounding fenland meet the style and sophistica-tion of modern city living.

CHESTER

Savour the historic delights of the Roman walls and charming black-and-white architec-ture, blending seamlessly with the contemporary shopping experience that make Chester such an exhilarating city.

EDINBURGH

Everyone falls in love with Edinburgh, with its Old and New Towns, where a lively café culture, fabulous shops and modern museums sit easily in ancient streets where bloody battles and royal pageant have played their part.

OXFORD

City and university life intertwine in Oxford, with its museums, bookstores and all manner of sophisticated entertainment to entice visitors to its hidden alleyways, splendid quadrangles and skyline of dreaming spires.

STRATFORD

Universally appealing, the picturesque streets of Stratford draw visitors back time and again to explore Shakespeare's birthplace, but also to relish the theatres and stylish riverside town that exists today.

YORK

A warm northern welcome and modern-day world-class shops and restaurants await you in York, along with its ancient city walls, Viking connections and magnificent medieval Minster rising above the rooftops.

Jarrold Publishing, Healey House, Dene Road, Andover, Hampshire, SP10 2AA, UK
Sales: 01264 409206 Enquiries: 01264 409200 Fax: 01264 334110
e-mail: customer.services@jarrold-publishing.co.uk website: www.britguides.com

HOVE CITY CENTRE

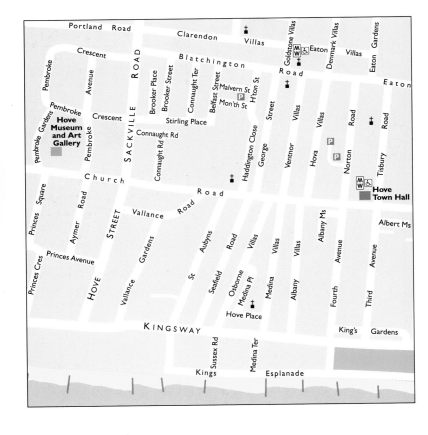